HIDDEN
HISTORY
of
WORCESTER

HIDDEN
HISTORY
of
WORCESTER

Dave Kovaleski

THE
History
PRESS

Published by The History Press
Charleston, SC
www.historypress.com

Front cover: Library of Congress Prints and Photographs Division.
Back cover, top: Lionel Pincus and Princess Firyal Map Division, The New York Public Library. "Underground routes to Canada." The New York Public Library Digital Collections; *bottom*: National Portrait Gallery, Smithsonian Institution.

First published 2021

Manufactured in the United States

ISBN 9781467149006

Library of Congress Control Number: 2021943540

Worcester Common with the Soldiers' Monument at center and City Hall in the
background. *Library of Congress Prints and Photographs Division.*

CONTENTS

PREFACE

From the American Revolution to the emancipation of slaves to the fight for women's rights, the city of Worcester, Massachusetts, and its people have been a catalyst for the seismic cultural and political shifts that shaped this nation in its first one hundred years. Simply put, the history of Worcester is the history of our nation.

Its narrative is told through patriots like Timothy Bigelow, who spearheaded a revolution to take back Worcester from British rule almost two years before the Declaration of Independence, and Isaiah Thomas, the founder of the groundbreaking newspaper the *Massachusetts Spy*, who was one of the first people to read the Declaration of Independence to a public audience—in Worcester.

There may be no one more influential in the Worcester story than Abby Kelley Foster, a reformer and pioneering voice against slavery and for women's rights who opened her home as a stop on the Underground Railroad and helped establish the first in a series of National Women's Rights Conventions in Worcester. Another central figure in the story of Worcester is Charles Allen, a Worcester congressman who helped form the anti-slavery Free Soil Party over the objections of a young congressman from Illinois named Abraham Lincoln, who visited Worcester to stump for Whig presidential candidate Zachary Taylor. Lincoln went back home to Illinois from his Worcester trip with his resolve more steeled than ever to end slavery.

And one of the most radical voices during the tumultuous years leading up to the Civil War was Pastor Thomas Wentworth Higginson, one of

John Brown's "Secret Six," who was one of the leaders of a raid on Boston to free a Black man who had been unjustly arrested. Higginson later commanded an all-Black brigade in the Civil War and fought alongside Colonel George Hull Ward, who died at Gettysburg, fighting for the Union with only one leg. Ward was just one of the Worcester-area heroes of the Civil War, along with the "angel of the battlefield," Clara Barton, who went on to form the American Red Cross. Worcester was also a pioneer in the world of sports, with one of the first professional baseball teams—the Worcester Brown Stockings, also known as the Worcesters and sometimes referred to as the Ruby Legs.

These stories seek to illuminate the people and events that laid the foundation on which the nation is built. Some of the nation-altering changes that sprang from Worcester in the first one hundred years of the republic may get lost in the shuffle of time, particularly outside of Worcester, but they should never be minimized or forgotten. A great deal of thanks goes to William Wallace, executive director of the Worcester Historical Museum, for his help and guidance with this book.

Here are the stories of the revolutionaries, reformers, pioneers and voices of change from Worcester who helped shape a nation.

I

THE WORCESTER REVOLUTION

The chain of events that led to the American Revolution is well documented, but one key conflict is often overlooked: the Worcester Revolution. Some seven months before Paul Revere's midnight ride to Lexington and almost two years before the Founding Fathers signed the Declaration of Independence, the people of Worcester County gained their independence from the British. It culminated with a peaceful show of force on Worcester Common on the morning of September 6, 1774, when the British surrendered the courts after being deposed at every level of local government. It was a battle for liberty, freedom and the soul of the fledgling nation, but it was not fought with guns or weapons, and not a drop of blood was shed, as Ray Raphael detailed in his groundbreaking book *The First American Revolution: Before Lexington and Concord*. It was fought with steely resolve and an unbending belief in what was right and just—and it inspired others to take up the fight.

To understand how the seeds of revolution were planted, it is necessary to go back some ten years earlier to the end of the French and Indian War. French and British settlers, each aided by Native American tribes, fought over territories throughout the New World. The war lasted from 1754 to 1763 and ended with a British victory, as France agreed to surrender its territories east of the Mississippi River to the English. The decade-long war had not only been brutal and bloody, but it had also been expensive. Fighting this war while managing the thirteen colonies left England cash-strapped and in debt.

As a result, the British Parliament imposed several new taxes on the colonists, including the Sugar Act of 1764 and the Stamp Act of 1765. The former put a tax on sugar imports, while the latter taxed colonists on all manner of printed paper, whether it was for newspapers, legal documents, playing cards or anything else. This inflamed the colonists, particularly those in Massachusetts, as William Sweetzer Heywood documented in *The History of Westminster, Massachusetts*, published in 1893.

> *Violent hostility to the measure was manifested in various parts of the country. The stamp distributor in Boston, Andrew Oliver, was hung in effigy. A building supposed to be his office was torn to pieces. The house of his brother-in-law, Chief Justice Thomas Hutchinson, afterwards governor, a strong supporter of kingly prerogative, was ransacked and stripped of its contents, while he and his family, hurrying out of town, barely escaped with their lives.*

To circumvent the taxes, the colonists informed the British that they would start manufacturing their own goods. This angered the British, who responded with more taxes via the Townshend Acts of 1767. These acts taxed items like glass, lead, paint, paper and tea imported to the colonies—items that the colonists would need in order to manufacture some of their own products. And the revenue, in part, would be used to pay the salaries of colonial governors and other leaders to ensure their loyalty to the Crown—a payoff, if you will. But the scheme backfired and sparked widespread protests and boycotts of British goods throughout the colonies. In Worcester, a selectman named Joshua Bigelow brought to the March 1768 town meeting a proposal to boycott goods manufactured by the British. The same thing was happening in Boston. Heywood called it the "unconquerable rage of the people."

To quell the unrest, the British dispatched about two thousand troops to Boston in 1769, but it only led to more protests. Tensions boiled over on March 5, 1770, when British soldiers killed five Americans and wounded six by shooting at an angry mob of protesters in Boston. The Boston Massacre happened on the very day that British prime minister Frederick North, unbeknownst on this side of the Atlantic, requested that Parliament repeal the Townshend Acts.

The British repealed all the taxes in the Townshend Acts except one, the tax on tea. But the Massachusetts colonists refused to abide by this dictum and boycotted tea imported by the British East India Company, the largest

A sensationalized portrayal of the Boston Massacre, March 5, 1770. *Library of Congress Prints and Photographs Division.*

merchant in the world, which had a royal charter from the Crown. Instead, the local colonists were able to get tea smuggled in from Dutch merchants, which struck hard at the British East India Company, putting it on the verge of bankruptcy. The British Parliament responded by passing the Tea Act in May 1773. This act allowed the company to sell tea to the colonies duty-free, undercutting other tea companies, but the British were still allowed to tax the tea when it reached colonial ports. The colonists were furious, particularly in Massachusetts. On December 16, 1773, frustrations came to a head at Griffin's Wharf in Boston. Colonists dumped 342 chests of tea—an entire shipment imported by the British East India Company— into Boston Harbor. This so-called Boston Tea Party became a flashpoint, signaling to the British that the colonists were fed up. It was the first open act of rebellion against the British, but it was just a start.

When news of the defiant act reached London, there was much outrage among the ruling party. Parliament retaliated against Massachusetts, passing several bills to punish the colony. These were known as the Intolerable Acts, or Coercive Acts, passed in 1774. One of them was the Boston Port Bill, which went into effect on June 1, 1774, and effectively closed Boston Harbor until restitution was made for dumping the tea.

Another, the Massachusetts Government Act (MGA), was by far the most egregious to most residents in the colony. It rescinded the colony's charter of 1691, reducing it to a Crown colony. A Crown colony was under direct authority of the British government and was no longer allowed to self-govern. So, not only was the governor appointed by the Crown, as was the case before, but now the colony's Executive Council was also Crown-appointed. The Executive Council, the upper body of the legislature, had previously served as a check and balance to the governor. In addition, all local officials, who were previously elected, were appointed by the British, and town meetings were limited to once per year, unless specific permission was granted by the governor.

These acts were meant to not only quash the rebellion in Massachusetts but also send a message to the rest of the colonies that insurgency would not be tolerated. But it had the opposite effect, as uprisings and protests sprang up throughout the colonies and here at home, particularly Worcester.

Townspeople from across Massachusetts were incensed by the Massachusetts Government Act, as it reached into their own backyards and revoked their right to a representative government. But it was the people of Worcester County in particular who took matters into their own hands.

First, it is helpful to understand how government in Massachusetts worked in those days. In Massachusetts, there were three legislative bodies in what was called the Massachusetts General Court. There was the House of Representatives, the Executive Council, and the governor's office.

The House of Representatives was made up of officials elected by their local communities. Each town elected at least one representative in the House, while larger towns were given two representatives. There was an upper legislative body called the Executive Council, which confirmed actions taken by the House and acted as advisor to the governor, approving the governor's appointments. The council was made up of twenty-eight seats, which were appointed each year by members of the House. Through the council, the people had a voice on the governor's appointees because only elected officials in the House were named to the council. The British Crown appointed the governor, as well as the various positions within the office, like judges, justices of the peace, tax collectors and sheriffs, but checks and balances were in place through the House and the council. This all changed in May 1774 under the Massachusetts Government Act.

Early in 1774, the British appointed a new governor, General Thomas Gage, the former commander in chief of the British forces in North America. Gage, who replaced Governor Thomas Hutchinson, was seen as more of an authoritarian, placed to help carry out the Intolerable Acts. One of Gage's first major acts was to install the new Executive Council, with all thirty-six members handpicked by King George III. Only three of them had been holdovers from the disbanded Executive Council, meaning they were elected by their peers. Another fourteen were former council members who were staunchly loyal to the Crown, and the rest were new appointees. Four of the Executive Council members were from Worcester—Timothy Paine, John Murray, Abijah Willard and Timothy Ruggles.

Not long before Gage was appointed, an opposition group began to form in Worcester called the American Political Society, or APS. It took shape in December 1773, forming out of the local Committee of Correspondence. The Committees of Correspondence was a network established in 1764 throughout the colonies to open lines of communication among those opposed to British rule. Each area had its own committee, including Worcester.

The Worcester APS was formed by local blacksmith Timothy Bigelow to fight the "machinations of some designing persons in this Province, who are grasping at power, and the property of their neighbors." Their ire was directed not only at the British, but also at the loyalists who ran Worcester for the British, namely John Chandler, John Murray, James Putnam and Timothy Ruggles, with the latter two serving on the Inferior Court of Common Pleas.

The APS had thirty-one original members and ultimately grew to more than seventy members, led by Bigelow, along with Samuel Curtis and Nathan Baldwin. The APS met once a month, and representatives attended every town meeting to voice their opinions and objections. At the town meeting in March 1774, one of their suggested resolutions was to not import British tea and to boycott anyone who sold it. Those who did should be considered traitors. When this was presented at the meeting by Timothy Bigelow, Putnam, a Tory, was livid, as were the other loyalists in charge. Putnam, Chandler (the town treasurer) and others signed a "desent and protest" against Bigelow and the APS for that resolution, which was entered into the town records.

At the next town meeting in April, the APS decried judicial salaries, calling them a bribe by the British to influence judges. The opposition had put great pressure on judges not to accept salaries throughout the colony; the only superior court judge who did was Chief Justice of the Superior Court of Massachusetts Peter Oliver from Boston. The Massachusetts House moved to impeach Oliver, but the matter was dropped after the former Massachusetts General Court was dissolved following the passage of the Massachusetts Government Act.

The APS led an effort to shut down the court if Oliver showed up at Worcester Superior Court as scheduled on April 19. Both Joshua Bigelow and Timothy Bigelow of the APS said they would refuse to sit on the grand jury, as scheduled, if Oliver showed up, according to William Lincoln's *History of Worcester*. Without grand jurors, it was impossible to hold court. Word reached Oliver of the situation, and he did not show up for court that day.

At the May Worcester town meeting, the APS began to exert more influence, as it now had several of its members on the town council, including William Young, Josiah Pierce and Benjamin Flagg. The town selectmen voted in favor of an APS proposal to provide instructions to the man they selected to voice Worcester's concerns to lawmakers in the new General Court in Boston, Joshua Bigelow, a cousin of Timothy Bigelow and a charter member of the APS. The instructions informed Bigelow to resist the "most distant approaches of slavery," oppose the Boston Port Bill, oppose providing compensation for the tea dumped in the harbor, work to convene a meeting of the Committees of Correspondence throughout the colonies and impeach Oliver, among other measures. Chandler, Putnam and the Tories—the political party loyal to the Crown—were incensed at the instructions and enraged that it actually passed, according to Lincoln's history.

The Tories immediately filed a petition against the motion and called for a meeting in June to reconsider it. But at that special meeting, the Tories were once again voted down—another sign that the winds of change were blowing in Worcester. Out of frustration, the Tory protesters, fifty-two of them, entered into the town records a motion expressing their dissent with the APS and the Committee of Correspondence. "These, and all such enormities, we detest and abhor. And the authors of them we esteem enemies to our King and country, violators of all law and civil liberty, the malevolent disturbers of the peace of society, subverters of the established constitution, and enemies of mankind," the motion said, according to Lincoln.

The Worcester Patriots would not stand for this startling rebuke. Just two months later, during the week of August 7, just days after Gage's new Executive Council officially took office, approximately fifty-two members of the APS and the local Committee of Correspondence convened at Stearns Tavern in what became known as the Worcester Convention.

In an opening address as captured in the *Journals of Each Provincial Congress of Massachusetts in 1774 and 1775*, Timothy Bigelow stated:

> *The committees of correspondence from a majority of towns in this county, have now convened at Worcester, in order to consult and determine upon the most regular steps to be taken and recommended to the several towns in this county, at this truly critical and alarming crisis, when it no longer remains a doubt, that the acts, annihilating our once free constitution, are actually come authenticated, attended with three more transports and a ship of war, and the council, appointed by his majesty, are about taking the oaths required for that office.*

Bigelow, along with Joshua Bigelow and John Smith of Worcester and seven others from surrounding towns—Ephraim Doolittle, Joseph Henshaw, Samuel Ward, Luke Drury, Edward Rawson, Paul Mandell and Jonathan Holman—drafted a resolution, as detailed in the *Journal*, that stated, in effect, that the passage of the Massachusetts Government Act would "destroy the allegiance we owe to the king," adding that it is the "indisputable duty of every American, and more especially in this province, to unite in every virtuous opposition that can be devised, in order to save ourselves and posterity from inevitable ruin."

It was, in essence, a declaration of independence. The call would soon go out to towns throughout Worcester County to adopt "some wise, prudent, and spirited measures, in order to prevent the execution of those most alarming acts of parliament, respecting our constitution." In other words, the Worcester Patriots were sending out word to take their own actions to thwart and subvert the effects of the Massachusetts Government Act.

One of the "spirited measures" was the Solemn League and Covenant, which called for a halt to the purchase of British goods. People were asked to sign the covenant and boycott those merchants who did not sign it. This rattled the Tories as well as local merchants, some of whom complained to the governor about acts of intimidation against them.

Also, some spirited measures were taken by the people of Worcester County against the new Crown-appointed members of the Executive

Council. Timothy Ruggles, from nearby Hardwick, received an ominous letter from Daniel Oliver, a friend back home from Hardwick, while Ruggles was being sworn into the council in Boston. "There are those here, who I am satisfied, thirst for your blood, and they have enough influence over the others to put them upon spilling it," Oliver wrote to Ruggles, according to the Colonial Society of Massachusetts. "High threats continue that you shall never pass the great Bridge alive, and all unite in the opinion that you will not be able to do it."

Ruggles was so terrified of the unrest in his district that he avoided going home, electing instead to stay with a friend in Dartmouth, Massachusetts. But ultimately, the friend demanded that Ruggles leave, knowing he was a Council Member and a marked man by some. So Ruggles decided to visit England rather than go home and face his angry constituents.

Abijah Willard, another Worcester-area member of the Executive Council, had an even worse reception among his constituents. Hearing about the unrest, Willard also decided against returning to his home in Lancaster, Massachusetts, after being sworn in. Willard opted instead to take a trip to Union, Connecticut. But his reputation preceded him, and Willard was apprehended in Union and thrown in jail at Newgate Prison in Simsbury, Connecticut. Shortly thereafter, on or about August 25, Willard was extradited back to Massachusetts, where he was met with an angry mob in the border town of Brimfield demanding he resign. They were so adamant that Willard resigned on the spot. According to the Massachusetts Historical Society, Willard wrote the following:

> *Whereas I, Abijah Willard, of Lancaster, have been appointed, by mandamus, a Counsellor for this Province, and having without due consideration taken the oath, do now freely and solemnly declare that I am heartily sorry that I have taken the said oath, and do hereby solemnly and in good faith promise and engage that I will not sit or act in the said Council, nor in any other that shall be appointed in such manner and form, but that I will as much as in me lies, maintain the Charter rights and liberties of this Province; and do hereby ask the forgiveness of all honest, worthy gentlemen that I have offended, by taking the above said oath; and desire this may be inserted in the publick prints.*

The mob was so angry that one of the locals who dared speak in support of Willard was tarred and feathered, according to the book *Tar, Feathers, and the Enemies of American Liberties* by Benjamin H. Irvin.

Willard was the first domino to fall, but others would follow as the tide had turned. The APS and Committees of Correspondence had essentially taken control of Worcester, having gained the majority on the town council. Joshua Bigelow had been elected to the town council in May, as had Samuel Curtis. And Nathan Perry had replaced Tory John Chandler as treasurer at the direction of the council. At a town meeting on August 22, Bigelow and the APS demanded that those fifty-two Loyalists who opposed them in June be forced to sign a document, apologizing to the town of Worcester, the local Committees of Correspondence and the state Committees of Correspondence for casting "cruel aspersions" upon them.

Of the fifty-two who protested, all but five—among them Putnam— signed the forced apology. A resolution was also passed calling for the town clerk to "obliterate, erase, and otherwise deface the said recorded protest and the names thereto subscribed, so that it may become utterly illegible and unintelligible," according to Duane Hamilton Hurd's *History of Worcester County*.

The revolution was indeed already underway but far from complete. While Willard resigned, there were still three local councilors who had to be dealt with. There was also the matter of the Inferior Court of Common Pleas, which was scheduled to meet on September 6.

The Worcester Patriots had taken firm control of the city government and had the full support of the county residents, who were increasingly enraged by the Intolerable Acts. Now they set their sights on the three local council members to reclaim the county's representation in colonial government. The first target was Timothy Paine, a Worcester selectman until he took his seat on the Executive Council. Paine lived on Boston Road, the main thoroughfare through town, which is now known as Lincoln Street in Worcester. Unlike some of his fellow appointees, he had not fled. In fact, Paine was at home on August 27 when some two thousand farmers and residents from throughout the county rode into Worcester and assembled on Worcester Common to demand his resignation. Paine himself described the scene in a letter to Governor Gage, as transcribed by the Colonial Society of Massachusetts.

> *The People began to assemble so early as seven o'clock in the morning, and by Nine, by the best computation, more than Two Thousand men were paraded on our Common. They were led into town by particular persons chosen for that purpose, many were Officers of the Militia, and marched in at the head of their companies. Being so assembled they chose*

a large Committee from the whole body, which Committee chose a Sub Committee to wait upon me, namely Joshua Bigelow, Edwd Rawson, Thomas Denny, John Goulding and Joseph Gilbert, (the three first were of the last House of Representatives) who came to my house, leaving the main body upon the Common.

Paine was then escorted to the common, where he was forced to publicly resign before the two thousand people waiting for him. They "would not be satisfied unless I appeared before them." It was truly a dramatic public resignation. It is worth noting that Paine would later be on the right side of history. After he was forced to resign, Paine fled to Nova Scotia but then returned home and was elected by the people of Worcester to serve in the General Council within the new American government in 1788.

The same day after Paine's public resignation, the Worcester Patriots marched to John Murray's house in nearby Rutland to force him to step down. The Worcester Committee of Correspondence, including Timothy Bigelow, Joshua Bigelow, Stephen Salisbury, David Bancroft, Jonathan Stone, William Young and John Smith, led a group of about one thousand people to Murray's house, according to Caleb Arnold Wall's *Reminiscences of Worcester.*

Murray had been in Boston since his swearing-in on the council, but word had spread that he returned home to Rutland. However, when the protesters arrived at Murray's house, he wasn't there. The Patriots took their message public, publishing an open letter to Murray in the Boston newspapers demanding he resign. The Worcester Patriots did not mince words, as Raphael detailed in his book *The First American Revolution: Before Lexington and Concord.* "As you have proved yourself to be an open Enemy to this Province...a large Number of Men from several Towns are assembled, who are fully determined to prevent your holding said Office as Counsellor, at the Risque of our Lives and Fortunes; and not finding you at Home, think proper to propose to your serious consideration: the following viz: That you make an immediate Resignation of your Office, as a Counsellor." Murray's short term on the Executive Council was effectively over, as he never returned home to Rutland.

Ruggles, the last of the four Executive Council members from Worcester, was also hiding out in Boston, having returned from a trip to London. Ruggles would not be welcomed back to his home in Hardwick, should he ever return. He never did, effectively giving up his seat.

The news had gotten to Governor Gage that his council was falling apart. According to *American Archives: Containing a Documentary History of the English*

Portrait of Worcester merchant and patriot Stephen Salisbury by Gilbert Stuart. Salisbury was a leader in the Worcester Revolution. *Library of Congress Prints and Photographs Division.*

Colonies in North America, in a September 2 letter to Lord Dartmouth, who was the secretary of state to the colonies, Gage explained how things had completely unraveled.

> *Your Lordship will know that the state, not of this Province only, but of the rest, is greatly changed since Mr. Hutchinson left America. Though I saw things were bad when I wrote from Salem, I found them much worse than I expected when I arrived here. Several of the new Counsellors who dwell at a distance, have fled from their houses, and been obliged to seek protection among the troops at Boston; in that number were Messrs. Ruggles, Edson, Leonard, and Murray.... The object of the people was to force them to give up their seats in Council, which has taken effect with Mr. Paine, who was seized and roughly treated. There are bad reports of Mr. Watson, though I have no news from him; but Mr. Willard was grievously mal-treated, first in Connecticut, where he went on business; and every township he passed through on his way home, in this Province, had previous notice of his approach, and ready to insult him; arms were put to his breast, with*

threats of instant death, unless he signed a paper, the contents of which he did not know or regard. He went home, after making me that report; but the news is, that a large body was marching to his house, in Lancaster, to force him to some other concessions.

Gage also noted that individual towns were assembling and electing their own representatives, spirited measures done irrespective of the Massachusetts Government Act. "Civil Government is near its end," Gage wrote to Dartmouth, as detailed in the *American Archives*, which published all of the letters during this period between Gage and Dartmouth.

Gage indicated in an August 27 letter to Dartmouth that it might be necessary to send in troops to protect the courts in Worcester, which were due to go into session on September 6. That seemed very unlikely, especially since Ruggles, who was scheduled to preside over the Inferior Court of Common Pleas, was in hiding in Boston. Gage wrote:

In Worcester they keep no terms; openly threaten resistance by arms; have been purchasing arms; preparing them; casting balls and providing powder; and threaten to attack any troops who dare to oppose them. Mr. Ruggles, of the new Council, is afraid to take his seat as Judge of the Inferiour Court, which sets at Worcester, on the 7th of next month; and I apprehend that I shall soon be obliged to march a body of troops into that township, and perhaps into others, as occasions happen, to preserve the peace.

The Inferior Courts of Common Pleas was an important legislative body to the people, particularly in rural areas. Each county had its own inferior court, including Worcester, where cases related to the collection of debt and disputes over possessions, land and boundaries were heard. The people were wary of the courts because they were run by the elite, like Ruggles and Putnam, who, the people feared, were not sympathetic to their plight and served the interests of the wealthy and powerful. A judge's ruling against a poor local farmer or landowner could send them to the poorhouse, so it was the branch of government that most impacted them.

On August 30, the Massachusetts Superior Court in Boston convened, with Chief Justice Oliver presiding, but the foreman, Ebenezer Hancock, and the jurors refused to be sworn in, rendering it impossible to hold court, according to the *American Archives*.

In a September 2 letter to Lord Dartmouth, Gage explained his "intention to send a body of troops to Worcester, to protect the Court there; and, if wanted, to send parties to the houses of some of the Counsellors, who dwell in that county." But he acknowledged that it might be an exercise in futility if the jurors refused to sit. "I mean, my Lord, to secure all I can by degrees; to avoid any bloody crisis as long as possible, unless forced into it by themselves, which may happen....Nothing that is said at present can palliate; conciliation, moderation, reasoning, is over; nothing can be done but by forcible means."

The people of Worcester County were on edge as the date to convene the Worcester court approached, as there had been talk that Gage might use force to keep the courts open on September 6. While the Worcester Patriots did not want violence, they made it clear that they would be ready to fight if Gage did indeed send in troops.

Unlike Boston, where the courts opened but the jurors refused to participate, the Worcester Patriots had no intention of even allowing the court to open. The plan had been in place for weeks as to how they would shut down the courts and reinstall the former government, as outlined by a Committee of Correspondence meeting on August 29 at the Worcester County Court House, courtesy of the *American Archives*: "Voted, That if there be an invasion, or danger of an invasion, in any town in this county, then, such town shall, by their Committee of Correspondence, or some other proper persons, send letters by post immediately to the Committees of the adjoining towns, who shall send to the other Committees in the towns adjoining them, that they all come properly armed and accoutred to protect and defend the place invaded."

The Worcester Patriots had shown their strength a few days prior, on September 1 and 2, when British soldiers were removing gunpowder from a magazine in the Boston area. But word spread quickly throughout the state that something more nefarious had happened. Rumors circulated that shots had been fired at the magazine and six people had been killed. The information soon reached Worcester County, and within a span of hours, some six thousand militiamen from Worcester County had assembled and were ready for battle. The troops began marching to Boston, but before they arrived, they learned that it was all a rumor—shots had not been fired, and no one had been killed. The Worcester militia returned home. But the speed with which they had assembled, and the sheer size of their volunteer regiment, served as a warning to Gage and the British Loyalists.

The Powder Alarm was a practice run, of sorts, for what would happen just a few days later, on the morning of September 6. Local militias from thirty-seven towns throughout Worcester County mobilized and marched

Worcester Common. On September 6, 1774, 4,622 Patriots marched on the common in the Worcester Revolution. *Library of Congress Prints and Photographs Division.*

into Worcester to protect the courthouse and ensure it did not open. They came from as far north as Royalston, near the New Hampshire border, and as far west as Athol. In all, 4,622 people marched on Worcester, with the most, 260, coming from Worcester itself, according to *The Diary of Rev. Ebenezer Parkman.* Parkman was a reverend from Westborough. Also, 220 came from Hardwick, 200 from Westborough, 210 from Grafton and 180 from Leicester.

Parkman wrote: "1774 September 5 (Monday). Another Town Meeting, upon our public Difficultys—they agree to go to Worcester tomorrow, as it is expected that all other Towns of this County will, to prevent the session of the Court under the new unconstitutional Establishment. 1774 September 6 (Tuesday). A great Company march with staves and Fife, under Capt. Maynard, to Worcester."

By then, the Worcester Patriots had been assured that Gage was not going to send in troops, so they were not armed, although some accounts indicate that some did carry guns. For the most part, they were marching with nothing more than staves and fifes, as Parkman indicated. Parkman wrote that, in all, 4,722 militiamen filled the Worcester Common and lined along Main Street all the way to the courthouse a half mile away. (Note that Parkman's diary says 4,722 militiamen assembled; other sources say 4,622).

Meanwhile, some of the leaders from the Committees of Correspondence and APS took over the courthouse, barricading themselves inside to prevent any of the judges from entering. About twenty-five judges and justices who were supposed to report for duty at the court that morning were denied entry to the courthouse and escorted to a nearby tavern owned by Daniel Heywood to wait while the Worcester County Convention, which was meeting at Timothy Bigelow's house across the street from the courthouse, decided on the next course of action, according to the *Journals of Each Provincial Congress of Massachusetts in 1774 and 1775.*

A few hours later, the justices emerged from Heywood Tavern, located at Main and Exchange Streets, walking hat in hand past the crowd of five thousand to six thousand that lined the road from the tavern to the courthouse. As they walked past the crowd, they publicly apologized for accepting the appointments and resigned their posts. A Tory witness said, according to Frank Moore's *Diary of the Revolution*: "At Worcester, a mob of about five thousand collected, and prevented the Court of Common Pleas from sitting, (about one thousand of them had fire-arms) and all drawn in two files, compelled Judges, Sheriffs, and gentlemen of the Bar, to pass them with cap in hand, and read their disavowal of holding Courts under the new Acts of Parliament, not less than thirty times in their procession."

Another account, in the *Journals of the Provincial Congress*, said there were six thousand people assembled that morning.

> On the invitation of the convention, the people of the county had assembled to the number of about six thousand. The companies of the several towns were under officers of their own election and marched in military order. Having been formed in two lines, when the arrangements were completed, the royalist justices, and officers, were compelled to pass through the ranks, pausing, at intervals, to read their declarations of submission to the public will. At evening, finding that no troops were on their way to sustain the judicial tribunals, whose constitution had been corrupted by the act of parliament, the great assembly dispersed peacefully.

The next day, September 7, the convention convened again to pass several resolutions requiring the judges to basically disavow their own appointment and install the courts and judges as they existed before the MGA was enacted—minus Messrs. Ruggles, Murray and James Putnam, as the *Journal*

A reenactment of the Worcester Revolution held on September 7, 2014, at Institute Park in Worcester. *Courtesy of Massachusetts Office of Travel and Tourism.*

detailed. The Worcester patriots had reclaimed the county courts. From that day on, the Worcester Convention would appoint its own judges and have its own representatives, both of whom would be accountable to the people.

In October of that year, Joshua Bigelow was elected by the people to be Worcester's representative in the General Court, while his cousin, Timothy Bigelow, was elected to serve in the new Massachusetts Provincial Congress, which was a new governing body led by John Hancock that replaced the provincial assembly. Timothy Bigelow was given his instructions by the committee representing the people of Worcester on how he should serve. And those instructions were, in essence, a declaration of independence for Worcester, as Albert Alonzo Lovell captured in his book *Worcester in the War of the Revolution.*

> *That if all the infractions of our rights, by acts of the British Parliament, be not redressed, and we restored to the full enjoyment of all our privileges, contained in the Charter of this Province, granted by their late Majesties, King William and Queen Mary, to a punctilio, before the day of your meeting, then, and in that case, you are to consider the people of this Province as absolved, on their part, from the obligation therein contained,*

and to all intents and purposes reduced to a state of nature; and you are to exert yourself in devising ways and means to raise from the dissolution of the old Constitution, as from the ashes of the Phoenix, a new form, wherein all officers shall be dependent on the suffrages of the people for their existence as such, whatever unfavorable constructions our enemies may put upon such procedure. The exigency of our public affairs leaves no other alternative from a state of anarchy.

Worcester County had struck a major blow for American independence, as author Ray Raphael described in his definitive account of the Worcester Revolution, *The First American Revolution: Before Lexington and Concord*. With his book, published in 2003, Raphael was the first to bring this important and overlooked chapter in American history to the fore.

In the late summer and early fall of 1774, the people of rural Massachusetts completely and forcibly overthrew the established government and set up their own. This was the first American Revolution....When the British staged their counterrevolutionary attack on Lexington and Concord, people lost their lives. That was the beginning of what became known as the Revolutionary War, but the actual revolution which triggered this military offensive succeeded without a body count.

Raphael continued, "Unfortunately, the telling of history often requires one."

2

The Declaration of Independence
in Worcester

The dramatic events that led to Worcester's independence set the dominos in motion throughout the colonies. While revolution was happening in Worcester, the First Continental Congress was convening in Philadelphia with delegates from twelve of the thirteen colonies. The Continental Congress—which met from September 5 to October 26, 1774—was formed after the British passed the Intolerable Acts.

The congress met in Philadelphia to determine how to respond to these punitive and aggressive acts by the British. The Continental Congress voted to boycott British trade and demand a repeal of the Intolerable Acts, among various other actions. Seven months later, Paul Revere made his famous midnight ride to warn that the British were coming, and the next day, the first shots in the Revolutionary War were fired at the Battle of Lexington and Concord on April 19, 1775. From there, the battles raged throughout the colonies as the American army fought the British for independence.

About a year later, the Continental Congress convened again, on June 7, 1776, to consider a bill brought to the floor by the representative from Virginia, Richard Henry Lee. The Lee resolution, seconded by John Adams of Massachusetts, called for the colonies to break free from British rule—a declaration of independence.

The measure was approved, and the congress appointed a group led by Adams, Thomas Jefferson and Benjamin Franklin to draft a formal Declaration of Independence. The Declaration of Independence was

Paul Revere on his midnight ride to warn the countryside that the British were coming. *The Miriam and Ira D. Wallach Division of Art, Prints and Photographs: Picture Collection, The New York Public Library.*

officially presented to Congress on June 28, and one week later, on July 4, 1776, it was adopted and signed by fifty-six delegates from the thirteen colonies. It read in part:

> *We, therefore, the Representatives of the united States of America, in General Congress, Assembled, appealing to the Supreme Judge of the world for the rectitude of our intentions, do, in the Name, and by Authority of the good People of these Colonies, solemnly publish and declare, That these United Colonies are, and of Right ought to be Free and Independent States; that they are Absolved from all Allegiance to the British Crown, and that all political connection between them and the State of Great Britain, is and ought to be totally dissolved; and that as Free and Independent States, they have full Power to levy War, conclude Peace, contract Alliances, establish Commerce, and to do all other Acts and Things which Independent States may of right do. And for the support of this Declaration, with a firm reliance on the protection of divine Providence, we mutually pledge to each other our Lives, our Fortunes and our sacred Honor.*

Upon the adoption of the declaration, riders on horseback were sent out the next day, July 5, to all thirteen colonies to deliver copies of the Declaration of Independence to the masses. The *Philadelphia Evening Post* got a copy and published it in its entirety on July 6. By Monday, July 8, Colonel John Nixon of the Philadelphia Committee of Safety read it aloud at the Pennsylvania State House before some area politicians and members of the local militia who had assembled.

The first public reading in Massachusetts was scheduled to happen on July 14 in Boston, but something happened on the way to Boston—the declaration made a stop first in Worcester. Enter Isaiah Thomas. Thomas was a printer and publisher from Boston who founded the *Massachusetts*

John Trumbull's painting of the Declaration of Independence being presented to the Congress. *U.S. Capitol. Public domain.*

Spy, a newspaper originally based in Boston that quickly became the voice of the revolutionaries and the Whigs, the political party that supported American freedom. Naturally, it was despised and detested by the Tories. According to *The Diary of Isaiah Thomas*:

> *The Spy soon became a power in the Massachusetts Bay, and some of the ablest writers in the colony contributed to its columns. Its bold and defiant tone drew widespread attention to the printer; and while the paper was being burned by the common hangman in North Carolina, and Mr. Thomas burned in effigy, applications came from the Whigs in all parts of the country, to set up presses. The hostility of the loyalists toward him was extreme; he was frequently threatened with violence, his name was placed on the list of the suspected, and his office was known as the "sedition factory."*

The *Spy* soon became the most popular newspaper not just in Massachusetts but also one of the most popular in the thirteen colonies. It had a circulation of about thirty-six hundred subscribers when most papers had between three hundred and six hundred. In 1774, Thomas was encouraged by some

Isaiah Thomas, publisher of the *Massachusetts Spy*, which moved its operation to Worcester during the Revolutionary War. *Library of Congress Prints and Photographs Division.*

prominent Worcester Whigs, including Timothy Bigelow and Joseph Warren, to start a similar paper there. Thomas obliged, launching the *Worcester Gazette* in early 1775. It was the ideological brethren of the *Massachusetts Spy*.

Initially, Thomas had every intention of running both papers, keeping his *Massachusetts Spy* in Boston. But, in the spring of 1775, it became too dangerous to continue publishing in Boston, as it was still the seat of Governor Thomas Gage, a staunch Loyalist. Thomas was, in essence, in enemy territory. So, Thomas put the *Massachusetts Spy* on hiatus early that spring just before the war broke out. But the *Spy* was just too valuable to the revolution to be silenced, so at the urging of John Hancock and the Worcester Whigs, Thomas moved his operation out to Worcester, where the British had no influence or authority, according to *The Diary of Isaiah Thomas*.

> He went back to Boston, packed up his presses and types, and on the 16th of April, with the aid of Gen. Joseph Warren and Colonel Timothy Bigelow, 'stole them out of town in the dead of night,' and sent them ahead to Worcester. He remained behind, assisted in giving the alarm on the night of the 18th, and was actively engaged in the fight on the following day. He arrived in Worcester on the 20th and set up his press in the cellar of Colonel Bigelow's house on Boston Road in what now is Lincoln Square.

The *Spy* relaunched in Worcester on May 3, 1775, and became an invaluable voice for the people throughout the Siege of Boston, which followed the Battle of Lexington and Concord, and during other battles that followed. Thomas and his team of writers were on the front, reporting from the battlefield and delivering other stories that were essential to the cause of American freedom.

When the Declaration of Independence was adopted on July 4, 1776, Thomas had been living in Londonderry, New Hampshire, working on another business venture. But he was frequently in Worcester to oversee operations at the *Spy*. Thomas just happened to be in Worcester on July 14 when the courier was coming through town carrying the Declaration of Independence to Boston. As luck would have it, Thomas happened to run into him. According to Charles Lemuel Nichols, in his biography of Thomas:

> *While visiting Worcester to watch over his business interests, Thomas saw a horseman enter town on July 14, 1776. Upon inquiry he found that the messenger was bearing to the commander-in-chief at Cambridge an official copy of the Declaration of Independence. Convincing him of his own sincerity and hastily copying this precious document, Thomas gathered his townsmen before the church, read the precious words while standing on the front steps, and caused them to be printed in the subsequent issue of the Massachusetts Spy.*

Thomas read aloud his transcribed version of the Declaration of Independence from the front steps of the Meeting House on Main Street in Worcester, the site of the Worcester City Hall on the common, according to Lovell in his book *Worcester in the War of the Revolution*. The account of the day, as published in the *Spy* on July 22, 1776, and as described in William Lincoln's history, provides the details of Thomas's historic reading.

> *On Monday last, a number of patriotic gentlemen of this town, animated with a love of their country, and to show their approbation of the measures lately taken by the Grand Council of America, assembled on the green near the liberty pole, where, after having displayed the colors of the thirteen Confederate Colonies of America, the bells were set ringing and the drums a beating; after which the declaration of Independence of the United States was read to a large and respectable body, among whom were the Selectmen and Committee of Correspondence assembled on the occasion, who testified their approbation by repeated huzzas, firing of musketry and cannon, bonfires and other demonstrations of joy.*

The actual signed Declaration of Independence ultimately made it to Boston on July 18, when Colonel Thomas Crafts read it from the balcony of the State House in Boston to the large crowd that assembled. It was the first time the actual document was read to the public in Massachusetts. But it was entirely fitting that Worcester residents heard those majestic words from Thomas's scribbled copy, since Worcester had first broken from British rule.

A portrait of Isaiah Thomas. *Miriam and Ira D. Wallach Division of Art, Prints and Photographs: Print Collection, The New York Public Library.*

Thomas, as a postscript, also published the *New England Almanac*, a book on the history of printing, and founded the American Antiquarian Society in 1812. The society was the first national historical society in the United States and is still operating today at 185 Salisbury Street in Worcester. The American Antiquarian Society is both a learned society and a major independent research library. It houses the largest and most accessible collection of books, pamphlets, broadsides, newspapers, periodicals, music and graphic arts material printed through 1876, as well as manuscripts and a substantial collection of secondary texts, bibliographies and digital resources and reference works related to all aspects of American history and culture before the twentieth century. The society was presented with the 2013 National Humanities Medal by President Barack Obama in a ceremony at the White House.

That is quite a legacy for Thomas, who died on April 4, 1831, and is buried at the Rural Cemetery at 180 Grove Street in Worcester.

3

Timothy Bigelow's Heroics
in the Revolutionary War

One of the heroes of the Worcester Revolution, Timothy Bigelow, the founder of the APS and Worcester's representative in the new Massachusetts Provincial Congress, also played a major role in the battle for American independence.

Bigelow was born in Worcester on August 12, 1739, and lived in the Pakachoag Hill section of town. He was the son of Daniel Bigelow, a farmer, and Elizabeth Whitney. As a child, he attended the first schoolhouse in Worcester in the area that would later become known as Lincoln Square, where his teacher was none other than John Adams, who would become the second president of the United States, according to the book *The First School House in Worcester*.

Adams was just nineteen years old when he came to Worcester in 1755 to teach grammar school. He came at the behest of Pastor Thaddeus Maccarty, who attended Harvard's graduation and met Adams there, offering him the job of schoolmaster. Adams, not sure yet what he wanted to do with his life, took the job and held it for three years. It was during this time in Worcester that he decided he wanted to become a lawyer. He studied law with none other than Judge James Putnam, the British Loyalist who would later preside over the Inferior Court of Common Pleas, only to be deposed by Timothy Bigelow and the Worcester Patriots. Adams actually lived with Putnam and his wife, Elizabeth, while he studied law under Putnam and taught school. According to Kenneth Moynihan's book *A History of Worcester, 1674–1848,*

Adams was not exactly the best schoolmaster the school had seen. He spent much of his time writing and deep in thought, no doubt pondering how he planned to change the world.

As a young man, Bigelow worked as a blacksmith's apprentice and later became a blacksmith himself. He married Anna Andrews, an heiress whose family did not want her marrying a tradesman. They eloped to Hampton, New Hampshire, and settled in a house built by his father-in-law, Samuel Andrews, on the Boston Road in the area later known as Lincoln Square, near the corner of Lincoln and Main. Bigelow built a blacksmith shop behind the house, and the Bigelows, with their six children, lived happily together. Of course, Bigelow would turn to politics and lead the Worcester Revolution. But after that, the blacksmith-turned-politician would become a soldier. In August 1774, he formed the Worcester Company of the Massachusetts Minutemen, a standing volunteer army that was prepared to fight at a minute's notice if need be.

The call to arms came several months later, on the morning of April 19, 1775, when a messenger came through Worcester shouting, "To arms! to arms! the war is begun!" Minutes later, Captain Bigelow's company assembled on the green and marched toward Sudbury to join the battle with the Continental army. By the time they arrived, the British army had already retreated to Boston. Bigelow's company, as well as a command led by Captain Benjamin Flagg of Worcester, stood on guard surrounding Boston as a show of force and strength, according to Charles Hersey's *Reminiscences of the Military Life and Sufferings of Col. Timothy Bigelow*.

The Massachusetts militia, also known as the Minutemen, was reorganized at Cambridge and ultimately was incorporated into the Continental army that summer. Bigelow was appointed to major, leading a regiment from Worcester. In September 1775, Major Bigelow volunteered his regiment to join an invasion of Quebec City led by Colonel Benedict Arnold, who was later charged with treason for first providing intelligence to the British, then switching sides and leading British troops against his own country.

But at one point, Arnold was a war hero. He was the head of a Connecticut militia that marched north to assist the Massachusetts Minutemen and the Continental army at the siege of Boston, which followed the attack at Lexington and Concord. While stationed at Cambridge with the Massachusetts militia, Arnold had the idea of attacking Fort Ticonderoga in Upstate New York at the confluence of Lake George and Lake Champlain. Arnold set off to join up with Ethan Allen and his Vermont militia, the Green Mountain Boys, to lay siege on Fort Ticonderoga. The British had only recently taken the fort from the French in the French and Indian War. Arnold knew it was poorly defended and was ripe for the taking.

On May 10, 1775, Arnold, Allen and their men silently rowed across Lake Champlain at night and seized the fort in a surprise attack. It was America's first offensive victory of the Revolutionary War and gave the Americans an important strategic hold in the region and a passageway to move north into Canada.

Arnold returned to Cambridge that summer a war hero. While there, he convinced the general of the Continental army, George Washington, to let him lead troops in an attack on Quebec City, moving up through Maine. The Second Continental Congress had convened just that May and authorized an invasion of Quebec. Arnold thought he could help the effort by attacking Quebec City.

Arnold and eleven hundred troops, including Bigelow's regiment from Worcester, marched north through the Maine wilderness in September 1775. It turned out to be a brutally difficult two-month trek, as roughly two hundred men died along the way and some three hundred turned back. Bigelow was ordered to scale a 4,145-foot mountain in Franklin County, Maine, to get what Arnold thought might be a view of Quebec City. Of course, they were too far away to see the city, but for his efforts, Bigelow's men declared that the peak should be named after him. That was indeed the case, as this mountain near the headwaters of the Kennebec River is called Mount Bigelow to this day.

The soldiers endured severe hardships and hunger. One account said they were forced to eat their camp dogs. On October 26, almost two months into the trip, Bigelow wrote a letter to his wife, expressing his fears and frustrations, according to Hersey.

I am at this time well, but in a dangerous situation, as is the whole detachment of the Continental army with me. We are in a wilderness nearly one hundred miles from any inhabitants, either French or English, and but about five days provisions on an average for the whole. We are this day sending back the most feeble and some that are sick. If the French are our enemies, it will go hard with us, for we have no retreat left. In that case there will be no alternative between the sword and famine. May God in his infinite mercy protect you, my more than ever dear wife, and my dear children, Adieu, and ever believe me to be your most affectionate husband, Timo. Bigelow.

Mount Bigelow in Maine, named after Revolutionary War hero Timothy Bigelow, who led his regiment north with Benedict Arnold to attack Quebec City. *Courtesy of Petersent. Wikimedia Commons. Public domain.*

Bigelow's division reached Quebec in November and met up with Arnold and the rest of the troops. Then, on the night of December 31, they attacked Quebec City, but it did not go as hoped. One of the division leaders, Richard Montgomery, was killed. Arnold shattered his leg but managed to escape. Bigelow was not so fortunate. He was captured and taken prisoner, remaining in captivity until August 1776. Where he was held is not clear, but Hersey wrote that it is believed that Bigelow was kept in the hold of an English prison ship and was subject to "severe treatment and cruelty."

After roughly seven months in prison, Bigelow and other American prisoners were released as part of a prisoner exchange. He was transported back home by ship and arrived in Worcester in September 1776, a year after he initially left for Quebec City. Bigelow immediately reentered the fight and in February was appointed colonel in the Fifteenth Regiment of the Massachusetts Line in the Continental army. Bigelow and his regiment—comprising primarily men from the Worcester area—marched north to fight under the command of General Horatio Gates with the Continental army at Saratoga. His company was instrumental in defeating the British at Saratoga and capturing General John Burgoyne. Burgoyne's defeat and the surrender of his nearly six-thousand-man army was considered the greatest victory of the Revolutionary War at that point.

"At this scene of blood and carnage, Col. Bigelow, with his regiment from Worcester, behaved with uncommon gallantry. It was said by our informant, who was on the spot at the time, that the 15th regiment, under the command of Col. Bigelow, was the most efficient of any on the ground," according to Hersey.

After the surrender of Burgoyne at Saratoga, Bigelow and his men marched to help General Washington near Philadelphia. The battle did not go well for the colonists, but Bigelow was recognized by none other than Washington himself. Hersey details that Washington told his men the following:

> *This, gentlemen officers, is Col. Bigelow, and the 15th regiment of the Massachusetts line under his command. This, gentlemen, is the man who vanquished the former royalists in his own native town. He marched the first company of minute men from Worcester at the alarm from Lexington. He shared largely in the sufferings of the campaign against Quebec and was taken prisoner there. After his exchange he raised a regiment in his own neighborhood, and joining the northern army under Gen. Gates, participated in the struggle with Burgoyne, and shares largely in the honor of that victory.*

The British, led by General Cornwallis, took possession of Philadelphia and chased the Americans back to Valley Forge. Bigelow and the American forces spent the brutal winter of 1777–78 living in mud huts at Valley Forge. They were cold, tired and hungry, and many soldiers succumbed to the conditions. Many others were demoralized and ready to go home rather than starve or freeze to death. Bigelow was instrumental in rallying the troops during this winter of discontent. He said: "Gentlemen, I have heard all the remarks of discontent offered here this evening, but as for me, I have long since come to the conclusion, to stand by the American cause, come what will. I have enlisted for life. I have cheerfully left my home and family. All the friends I have, are the friends of my country. I expect to suffer with hunger, with cold, and with fatigue, and, if need be, I expect to lay down my life for the liberty of these colonies."

Word spread of the hardships at Valley Forge, and reinforcements soon arrived in the form of food, clothing, money and more troops as Marquis de Lafayette arrived with his French troops and General Gates with the rest of the northern army. In the spring, the American army moved back across the Delaware to New Jersey to engage in the Battle of Monmouth. It was at Monmouth where General Charles Lee, Washington's second in command, disobeyed orders from Washington and ended up retreating from the British brigade.

Colonel Bigelow was under the command of the other general in the Battle of Monmouth, General Lafayette. Lafayette's brigade was left in a precarious position but fought valiantly against great odds, only to ultimately retreat. But Bigelow's regiment was the last to exit the battlefield. One of his men, Solomon Parsons of Worcester, said Bigelow "fought more like a tiger than like a man." The American forces regrouped under the command of Washington and came back and drove the British into retreat.

After Monmouth, Bigelow and his regiment were dispatched to Robinson's Farms, New Jersey, to break up a group of Tories who were providing the English with food and supplies. Bigelow had been incensed by a recent attack in Wyoming, Pennsylvania, near Wilkes-Barre, where a group of Tories, allied with a Native American tribe, attacked an American fort and slaughtered the men inside. The Americans had been outnumbered, as many were off fighting in the war. It was a bloody massacre, and the gory details filled Bigelow with horror. He swore vengeance, reportedly telling a friend, "Our worst enemies are those of our own household."

At Robinson's Farms, the English had troops to help remove hay they were receiving from local Tories. Bigelow arrived to break it up and demanded they leave. Both the English soldiers and the local Loyalists initially refused, so Bigelow ordered his men to fire on them. The English fled.

From there, Bigelow's regiment was deployed to Verplank's Point, New York, on the Hudson River, where the British stormed Fort Lafayette by land and river. Colonel Bigelow fought to the bitter end, but the Americans were overpowered and had to surrender the fort. Some of the American troops were ordered to march south to serve under the command of General Gates. Initially, Colonel Bigelow had stayed behind to monitor the movement of the British in the New York region, but upon hearing that Gates's army was getting routed in the Carolinas, Bigelow also migrated south to help General Nathanael Greene, who had taken over the command. But by the time Bigelow and his men arrived, the battle had been lost.

After their victory, the British army moved north to encamp at Yorktown, Virginia. Bigelow and the rest of the American troops followed, laying siege to the British at Yorktown. The British would, of course, surrender on

October 19, 1781, and American independence was achieved. And Bigelow was there, on the front lines. "Why, old Col. Tim was everywhere all the time, and you would thought; if you had been there, that there was nobody else in the struggle but Col. Bigelow and his regiment," one of his men said, according to Hersey's book.

After four years of fighting from Quebec to Virginia, Bigelow eventually returned home to Worcester, but not before being stationed at West Point to help protect that installation in case of British retaliation, and then Springfield, where he oversaw the protection of a national arsenal. Finally, in November 1782, at the age of forty-three, Bigelow returned home.

Bigelow received a hero's welcome from family, friends and the entire Worcester community. But it was difficult to reacclimate to civilian life. His body had been through hardships that most men could never imagine, let alone live through. He was not only physically impaired but also financially strapped from having been away for so long. Debts had piled up, and he had not received his back military pay. Instead, Congress paid him in land, granting him 23,040 acres in Vermont in the area that is now Montpelier. But it was of little use to Bigelow, who needed to make money and didn't have any desire or the wherewithal to relocate to Vermont. He never actually received the grant for the land before he died, but historians say he did name the city, Montpelier, which would become the capitol of Vermont.

Bigelow went back to work in his blacksmith shop. However, he was in ill health and not able to earn enough to pay off his debt. His skills had diminished as a blacksmith, and other shops had emerged since he left, so it was difficult to reestablish himself. To make things worse, in 1787, Bigelow's second-oldest son, Andrew, died of consumption. Bigelow became distraught and depressed.

With debts he couldn't repay, a broken will and a battered body, Bigelow was thrown into debtors' prison at the Worcester County Jail. He died in prison after only six weeks there on March 31, 1790. He was only fifty-one years old. The prison record said he was discharged on April 1 "by Deth," according to the Bigelow Society. It was a sad end for perhaps the finest man and greatest hero that Worcester ever produced.

The house that Bigelow lived in is no longer there, as it was torn down in 1824. But there is a memorial honoring him on the Worcester Common. There is also a plaque put up by the Daughters of the American Revolution on Route 27 north of Stratton, Maine, commemorating his heroics on the Arnold Expedition. Incidentally, the Colonel Timothy Bigelow Chapter of the Daughters of the American Revolution is currently headquartered in

Colonel Timothy Bigelow Monument, located on the Worcester Common. *Courtesy of Daderot. Wikimedia Commons.*

a house on 140 Lincoln Street that was built by Timothy Paine, the British Loyalist and one of the four Crown-appointed Executive Council members that Bigelow and the rest of the APS forced to resign. The house, known as the Oaks, is listed in the National Register of Historic Places.

Just down the street from where Bigelow lived stood the home of another Worcester reformer, Stephen Salisbury. Salisbury, along with Bigelow, was one of the founders of the American Political Society. He moved to Worcester in 1767 from Boston, where his brother Samuel ran a store with goods imported from England and the West Indies. Stephen was sent to Worcester to open a store there, and S&S Salisbury was born.

Salisbury built his store and home on the former Boston Road, in the area now known as Lincoln Square, in 1772. He bought the land for the mixed-use property from John Hancock, the great Patriot who would become the first governor of Massachusetts, the first signer of the Declaration of Independence, and the president of the Second Continental Congress, according to the American Antiquarian Society. The Salisbury Mansion is still standing today, but it has since been moved a few blocks away to 40 Highland Street, at the back end of the Worcester Art Museum. It is listed in the National Register of Historic Places and is a historic house museum that is open to the public.

S&S Salisbury became the most popular store in the region and a center of commerce. It made Salisbury a very wealthy man. Salisbury ran the store well into his seventies before closing it in 1820. He continued to live at the house until he died on May 11, 1829, at the age of eighty-three. His wife, Elizabeth, who was twenty-one years younger than him, lived there until she died in 1851, also at eighty-three.

After Elizabeth died, the Salisbury Mansion served a variety of different owners, including a girls' school, a tenant house, a social club and a boys' club. In the 1920s, at a time when Lincoln Square was being developed, a group of Worcester residents purchased the mansion and storehouse and moved it to Highland Street, next to the Salisbury House, the home that Stephen and Elizabeth's son Stephen II built in 1836. Stephen Salisbury II was a prominent businessman, politician and the president of the American Antiquarian Society in Worcester. The Salisbury House is listed in the National Register of Historic Places.

The Salisbury Mansion in Worcester, home of Stephen Salisbury and his store, S&S Salisbury. *Library of Congress Prints and Photographs Division.*

4

LEVI LINCOLN, QUOCK WALKER AND THE END OF SLAVERY IN MASSACHUSETTS

No issue dominated the discourse of the day following the American Revolution, certainly in Worcester, more than slavery. Worcester had always been staunchly anti-slavery, dating as far back as 1767, when residents instructed their representatives in the Massachusetts General Court to "use your influence to obtain a law to put an end to that unchristian and impolitic practice of making slaves in this Province."

To illustrate how virulently anti-slavery Worcester County was, representatives from the county voted against the U.S. Constitution 43–7 because it contained no mention or statement on slavery, according to author Charles Nutt, the former publisher of the *Massachusetts Spy*, in his book *The History of Worcester and Its People*. As it turned out, the Constitution was only ratified in Massachusetts by the vote of 187–168 on February 6, 1788, per the Massachusetts Historical Society.

Worcester County delegates thought opposition to slavery should be included in the U.S. Constitution because it was already effectively abolished in the state of Massachusetts through the Massachusetts State Constitution, which had been ratified in 1780. One man who was instrumental in making that happen was one of Worcester's most prominent citizens, Levi Lincoln Sr.

Lincoln was born on May 5, 1749, in Hingham, Massachusetts, but the family moved to Worcester in his youth. Lincoln was an apprentice to an ironsmith, but he was a brilliant young man and was more drawn to books than to the anvil. He studied in his free time and was able to attend Harvard

University, graduating in 1772. He had planned to go into the ministry, but Lincoln, by chance, visited the Worcester courts one day when John Adams, the future president and former Worcester schoolteacher, was arguing a case. Lincoln was floored by Adams's eloquence and oratory, and it inspired him to change his career choice and become a lawyer. He studied law with Daniel Farnham of Newburyport and then Joseph Hawley of Northampton and soon became a jurist, according to Nutt.

In April 1775, Lincoln put his legal career on hold to march with Timothy Bigelow and the Worcester Minutemen to Cambridge when the British attacked Lexington and Concord. He did not see action, as the British had already retreated to Boston. Lincoln then returned to Worcester and opened a law practice. At this point, the courts had not yet reopened, having been shut down after the Worcester Revolution on that fateful day, September 6, 1774. Further, only two lawyers were in practice—John Sprague of Lancaster and Joshua Upham of Brookfield—as the Loyalists had all fled. This created an opportunity for Lincoln, and he took advantage of it, building what would become the largest practice in the county.

However, his practice did not keep him from public life. He had become active with the local Patriots, befriending members of the local Committee of Correspondence and advocating for the cause of independence in speeches, written statements and printed communications. When the courts reopened in December 1775, Lincoln was appointed clerk of the Court of Common Pleas for the County of Worcester. Then, in 1777, he was commissioned by the Executive Council to the position of judge of probate, an office he held until 1781. It was during this time that he met a man named Quock Walker.

Walker was born in 1753 in Massachusetts to Mingo and Dinah Walker, who were from Ghana. When Quock was about nine months old, the Walker family was bought into slavery by James Caldwell of Barre, Massachusetts, a town just west of Worcester. Caldwell told Quock that when he reached the age of twenty-five, he would be a free man. But Caldwell suffered an unfortunate accident on July 18, 1763, when he was caught outside during a storm. Lightning struck a tree in the yard and it fell on Caldwell, killing him. The Walker family then fell under the ownership of Caldwell's widow, Isabel, who, according to Quock, promised him his freedom at age twenty-one.

In 1765, when Quock was twelve, his father, Mingo, fled the Caldwell homestead to his freedom, leaving Quock with his mother and two siblings. Four years later, on March 28, 1769, the widow Isabel married a man named Nathaniel Jennison, who also, according to Quock, promised the young man's freedom at twenty-one. But in 1774, just before Quock turned twenty-one, Isabel died, and ownership of Quock and his family transferred over to Jennison. To Quock's dismay, Jennison allegedly went back on his promise to Quock and denied him his freedom.

Quock continued to serve as Jennison's slave for several years and formed a kinship with the Caldwell sons, Seth and John. In April 1781, Quock decided to leave Jennison to go work for Seth and John as a free man on their farm. The Caldwell brothers had urged Quock to come work for them after getting legal consultation from the noted Worcester attorney Levi Lincoln.

On the day that Quock left, Jennison showed up at the Caldwell farm, demanding that Quock return "home." Quock refused, but Jennison returned once again on May 1 and tried to take Quock by force. He brought along two men, who apprehended Quock while he was working in the fields and pinned him to the ground. One of the Caldwell brothers heard the screaming and came to Walker's rescue. Caldwell tried to pull the men off Walker, but he was overpowered, and Jennison and his men carried Walker away. The Caldwell brothers followed Walker back to Jennison's farm and found Walker locked in the sawmill, savagely beaten, according to an account in *Historical Digression: Quock Walker and Emancipation in Massachusetts* by Patrick Browne.

The Caldwells demanded that Walker be set free, citing the promise made by their deceased parents, but Jennison refused. But Walker would not be denied. With the encouragement and guidance of the Caldwell brothers, Walker sued Jennison for assault and battery. The complaint called it "trespass for an alleged assault and beating of plaintiff by defendant with a hoe-handle," as well as fists, as Abijah Marvin wrote in his *History of Worcester County*.

Walker retained the legal services of Lincoln and his fellow Worcester attorney Caleb Strong to represent him in the case, *Walker v. Jennison*, heard in the Worcester Court of Common Pleas on June 12, 1781. Jennison's attorneys, John Sprague and William Stearns, argued that Walker was the rightful property of Jennison and, as such, Jennison could do as he pleased. The attorneys produced the bill of sale as proof of ownership. Lincoln and Strong countered by saying the original owner, James Caldwell, had promised Walker his freedom at age twenty-five, therefore, since he was now twenty-eight, he was a free man and was injured without right. The jury agreed, ruling "that the said Quork [*sic*] is a Freeman and not the proper Negro slave of [Jennison]." Walker was awarded sixty pounds in damages plus legal costs, according to Marvin.

A second case associated with this incident turned out to be far more historically significant. On the same day that *Walker v. Jennison* was heard, so was *Jennison v. John and Seth Caldwell*. Jennison sued the two brothers for "enticing away his slave, Quork Walker, and rescuing him out of his (Jennison's) hands." Jennison also sued for "depriving him (Jennison) of the services of his servant," as Abijah Marvin wrote in his *History of Worcester County*. The court ruled in favor of Jennison, but while he sought one thousand pounds in damages, he was awarded only twenty-five. The Caldwell brothers, who were also represented by Lincoln and Strong, appealed the decision to the Massachusetts Superior Court of Judicature. As they did in *Walker v. Jennison*, Lincoln and Strong argued that Walker was not a slave or property of Jennison but a free man. In his argument before the jury and Massachusetts Supreme Court chief justice William Cushing, Lincoln spoke of the evils of slavery and how it was against the laws not only of man but also of God.

He argued, as detailed by the Massachusetts Historical Society in *Proceedings of the Massachusetts Historical Society* (Volume 6):

In making out that negroes are the property of their masters, the counsel for the plaintiff speak of lineage, and contend that the children of slaves must be slaves in the same way that, because our first parents fell, we all fell with them. But are not all mankind born in the same way? Are not their bodies clothed with the same kind of flesh? Was not the same breath of life breathed into all? We are under the same gospel dispensation, have one common Saviour, inhabit the same globe, die in the same manner; and though the white man may have his body wrapped in fine linen, and his attire may be a little more decorated, there all distinction of man's making ends. We all sleep on the same level in the dust. We shall all be raised by the sound of one common trump, calling unto all that are in their graves, without distinction, to arise; shall be arraigned at one common bar; shall have one common Judge, and be tried by one common jury, and condemned or acquitted by one common law, by the gospel, the perfect law of liberty. This cause will then be tried again, and your verdict will there be tried.

Lincoln concluded his argument by asking the jury:

Is it not a law of nature, that all men are equal and free? Is not the law of nature the law of God? Is not the law of God, then, against slavery? If there is no law of man establishing it, there is no difficulty. If there is, then the great difficulty is to determine which law you ought to obey; and, if you

5

[*Charge of the Chief Justice.*]

" *Fact proved.*

"Justification that Quack is a slave — and to prove it 'tis said that Quack, when a child about 9 months old, with his father and mother was sold by bill of sale in 1754, about 29 years ago, to Mr. Caldwell, now deceased; that, when he died, Quack was appraised as part of the personal estate, and set off to the widow in her share of the personal estate; that Mr. Jennison, marrying her, was entitled to Quack as his property; and therefore that he had a right to bring him home when he ran away; and that the defendant only took proper measures for that purpose. And the defendant's counsel also rely on some former laws of the Province, which give countenance to slavery.

" To this it is answered that, if he ever was a slave, he was liberated both by his master Caldwell, and by the widow after his death, the first of whom promised and engaged he should be free at 25, the other at 21.

" As to the doctrine of slavery and the right of Christians to hold Africans in perpetual servitude, and sell and treat them as we do our horses and cattle, that (it is true) has been heretofore countenanced by the Province Laws formerly, but nowhere is it expressly enacted or established. It has been a usage — a usage which took its origin from the practice of some of the European nations, and the regulations of British government respecting the then Colonies, for the benefit of trade and wealth. But whatever sentiments have formerly prevailed in this particular or slid in upon us by the example of others, a different idea has taken place with the people of America, more favorable to the natural rights of mankind, and to that natural, innate desire of Liberty, with which Heaven (without regard to color, complexion, or shape of noses) features) has inspired all the human race. And upon this ground our Constitution of Government, by which the people of this Commonwealth have solemnly bound themselves, sets out with declaring that all men are born free and equal — and that every subject is entitled to liberty, and to have it guarded by the laws, as well as life and property — and in short is totally repugnant to the idea of being born slaves. This being the case, I think the idea of slavery is inconsistent with our own conduct and Constitution; and there can be no such thing as perpetual servitude of a rational creature, unless his liberty is forfeited by some criminal conduct or given up by personal consent or contract.

" *Verdict guilty.*"

A summary of Chief Justice Cushing's verdict in the so-called Quock Walker case. *Gray, Horace, and African American Pamphlet Collection.*

shall have the same ideas as I have of present and future things, you will obey the former. The worst that can happen to you for disobeying the former is the destruction of the body; for the last, that of your souls.

Lincoln also pointed out that slavery was prohibited, according to the Massachusetts Constitution, which had been ratified just one year prior in 1780. Article I of the Constitution said: "All men are born free and equal, and have certain natural, essential, and unalienable rights; among which may be reckoned the right of enjoying and defending their lives and liberties; that of acquiring, possessing, and protecting property; in fine, that of seeking and obtaining their safety and happiness."

This time, the jury voted in favor of the Caldwell brothers, swayed by Lincoln's impassioned argument. In effect, the courts determined that Walker was a free man, not owned by Jennison, and that they had the right to employ him. This case, and Lincoln's argument, all but ended slavery in Massachusetts even though it did not become illegal by act of the Massachusetts General Court until 1865. But it was deemed unconstitutional in the state, and the Quock Walker case set precedent for future legal cases.

Incidentally, Lincoln was one of the framers of the Massachusetts Constitution, which had been ratified the previous year on June 15, 1780. Lincoln was among three men selected from Worcester, along with David Bigelow and Joseph Allen, to attend the constitutional convention in Cambridge. Lincoln and the Worcester contingent worked with former Worcester schoolteacher and future president John Adams, who was also one of the delegates.

These were just the early days of Lincoln's legendary career. Around the same time, Lincoln bought a home on Boston Road in the current Lincoln Square area, a house formerly owned by the Honorable John Hancock, according to Wall's *Reminiscences of Worcester*. Hancock, who made his main residence in Boston, owned a second home in Worcester. He also owned, for a time, the Hancock Arms Tavern, near the courthouse, according to Lovell's *Worcester in the War of the Revolution*. It became the favorite watering hole of the Worcester Patriots leading up to the American Revolution, wrote John Paul Spears in *Old Landmarks and Historic Spots of Worcester, Massachusetts*. It was also a gathering place for the local militia members involved in Daniel Shays's rebellion before they marched into Springfield in 1787 in a failed effort to seize the Springfield Armory and overthrow the fledgling government over high taxes.

John Hancock did not make Worcester his principal residence, but he did stay at his Worcester home on occasion, particularly in the summer. His most historically notable stay at his Worcester home occurred in April 1775, after the British attacked Lexington and Concord. Hancock had been staying in Lexington at the time of the attack with fellow Patriot Samuel Adams. He wanted to stay and fight, but Adams and others prevailed upon him the need to leave, as the British were looking for him, and his leadership would be essential in the coming war. After leaving Lexington, Hancock and Adams eventually made their way out to Worcester on April 24 to stay at the Hancock mansion. From Worcester, Hancock wrote a letter to the Massachusetts Provincial Congress, of which he was president, to inform them of his whereabouts and his plans to head to Philadelphia for the Second Continental Congress.

While in Worcester, he was also awaiting the security of a trunk filled with important papers that Paul Revere, after his famous midnight ride, was going to secure. The trunk had been left at Buckman Tavern in Lexington Center. Hancock was not able to bring it with him, but he asked his clerk, John Lovell, to rescue it, as it contained sensitive documents related to the cause that would be devastating if they fell into the hands of the British. The trunk—about four feet long by two feet wide by two and a half feet high—was extremely heavy, filled as it was with documents. It could not be carried by Lovell alone. Lovell sought out Revere to help him take it out of the tavern. Initially, they were only able to drag it into the woods, as the attack had begun. Ultimately, the trunk was secured and brought out to Hancock in Worcester, and it remained in his possession as he traveled to Philadelphia to attend the Continental Congress. As a postscript, this trunk ultimately did make it back to Worcester, when it was donated by a descendant, minus the important papers, to the American Antiquarian Society, which in turn donated it to the Worcester Historical Museum.

Levi Lincoln bought Hancock's former home around 1782. At that time, it had been used as a boardinghouse run by Samuel Woodburn. According to Lovell's book, "the grounds connected with this estate were considered the finest in the town." Lincoln lived there until he died in 1820. The house was moved to Grove Street in 1846 and was razed in 1920, but the doorway was saved and sits in the Smithsonian Institution in Washington, D.C.

After the landmark Quock Walker case, Lincoln was conferred by the Massachusetts Supreme Court the degree of barrister-at-law, the highest honor an attorney can achieve. Only a handful of others earned this distinction, including the previously mentioned Strong and Sprague.

"He was, without question, at the head of the bar, from the close of the Revolution till he left our courts at the commencement of the present century," said Worcester attorney Joseph Willard, speaking about Lincoln at a meeting of the Worcester County Bar on October 2, 1829, as published in the *New England Historical and Genealogical Register*.

His professional business far exceeded that of any other member of the bar. He was retained in every case of importance, and for many years, constantly attended the courts in Hampshire and Middlesex (and frequently those of the neighboring states). His great command of language, his power in searching out the truth from unwilling witnesses, in analyzing, arranging, and presenting to the mind the evidence of the case, rendered him a highly popular advocate, and gave him great success in jury trials.

In 1796, Lincoln turned to politics and was elected to the Massachusetts House of Representatives, the state's legislative body. He then served in the state senate in 1797. Lincoln served with distinction and was influential in shepherding major modifications to both the judicial and school systems in the state. Lincoln had run for a seat in Congress several times in the 1790s but was defeated every time by Dwight Foster. When Foster moved over to the U.S. Senate in 1800, Lincoln finally won a seat in the U.S. House of Representatives, serving the Fourth District of Massachusetts. His tenure there was short-lived, as new president Thomas Jefferson appointed Lincoln as U.S. attorney general on March 5, 1801. He was also acting secretary of state for Jefferson until May 1, 1801, when James Madison filled the role.

Lincoln served as attorney general for Jefferson's first term until March 3, 1805. He decided not to serve a second term so that he could be back with his growing family in Worcester. Jefferson was disappointed but understood, as he outlined in a letter to Lincoln dated December 28, 1804, and held in the Library of Congress.

I received last night your letter, proposing to resign your office; and I received it with real affliction. It would have been my greatest happiness to have kept together to the end of my term our executive family; for our harmony and cordialty have really made us but as one family. Yet, I am a father, and have been a husband. I know the sacred duties which these relations impose; the feelings they inspire; and that they are not to be resisted by a warm heart. I yield, therefore, to your wishes. You carry with you my entire approbation of your official conduct, my thanks for your services, my regrets on losing them, and my affectionate friendship.

While he was done with national politics, Lincoln remained active locally. In the spring of 1806, he was appointed to the Governor's Council, a body that advised the governor. The next year, 1807, he was nominated to serve as lieutenant governor of the commonwealth under Governor James Sullivan. But Sullivan died while in office on December 10, 1808, and Lincoln became governor. He served in the capacity only until May 1, 1809, when Sullivan's term ended. Lincoln ran for another term but lost to Christopher Gore. Lincoln again served on the Governor's Council after that defeat in 1810 and 1811. In 1811, he was approached by President James Madison to serve as associate justice on the U.S. Supreme Court. Madison wrote to Lincoln, per the Library of Congress:

You will see by the commission which will be forwarded from the Department of State, that I have taken the liberty of nominating you to the Senate as successor to Judge Cushing, notwithstanding your remonstrances against a recall into the national service. I was induced to this step, not only by my personal wishes, but by those of others, between whom and yourself exists all the reciprocal respect that can add weight to them, and particularly by their persuading themselves, that your patriotism would acquiesce in an appointment, however contrary it might be to your previous inclinations. I venture to flatter myself that in this we may not be disappointed: and that, in every event, you will regard the liberty I have taken in imposing the dilemma upon you, with the indulgence due to my motives, and to the great esteem and sincere friendship of which I pray you to accept my renewed assurances.

The Cushing he referred to was William Cushing, the former Massachusetts Supreme Court justice that Lincoln argued the Quock Walker case before. Cushing was later appointed to the U.S. Supreme Court by George Washington in 1790 and died in 1810, leaving a vacancy. However, Lincoln respectfully declined the offer, citing his failing eyesight. At that point, Lincoln was mostly retired from public life but was a founding member of the American Antiquarian Society in 1812 and the first president of the Worcester Agricultural Society in 1818. Lincoln died on April 14, 1820, and is interred at the Worcester Rural Cemetery.

As Nutt detailed in his book, Lincoln's obituary in the April 26, 1820 issue of the *Spy* captured his profound legacy.

How few of our rising politicians have been taught that the first practical comment on the introductory clause of the Bill of Rights was first given by a Worcester jury; that it was here first shown by the irresistible eloquence of Lincoln that all men were in truth born free and equal, and that a Court sitting under the authority of our constitution could not admit as a justification for an assault, the principle of master and slave; that it was the memorable verdict obtained upon this trial which first broke the fetters of negro slavery in Massachusetts and let the oppressed go free. This deed of Judge Lincoln, even if it stood alone, ought to consecrate his memory with every freeman.

5

ABBY KELLEY FOSTER AND THE
UNDERGROUND RAILROAD

In the formative years of the republic, after independence was won, an age of ideas emerged in the tumultuous years leading up to the Civil War. New thoughts on religion, government, human rights, business, education, temperance and culture emerged as the nation began to define its identity. This created a melting pot of differing viewpoints that led to robust discussions, heated debate and major societal change. The era between 1840 and the Civil War was truly an age of reform in these young United States.

It was not just in the big cities where these debates were happening. Many smaller towns throughout the region established lyceums at meetinghouses, where these ideas were aired and hotly debated in public by the people. Worcester, as it was during the American Revolution, was at the center of these debates and in many ways was the beating heart of change. Abolitionist Thomas Wentworth Higginson, a Worcester pastor who was one of John Brown's "Secret Six," called the city the "seething centre of all reforms," according to the Worcester Historical Museum—not just in the state, but nationally, as Worcester was leading the way on many of these critical issues of the day.

In *The History of Worcester, Massachusetts*, J.W. Lewis wrote:

> *No period in the history of our nation since the Revolution has approached in the magnitude of the issues to be determined the years from 1848 to 1865. Political questions were dignified into the loftiest moral issues. The grandest fearlessness of political action was the result of the deepest*

ANTI-SLAVERY MEETING ON THE COMMON.

Antislavery meetings like this one depicted on Boston Common were popular throughout Worcester County in the 1840s. *General Research Division, The New York Public Library. "Anti-Slavery Meeting on the Common." The New York Public Library Digital Collections. 1851-05-03.*

convictions of the human soul. Deep answered unto deep, and heart to heart. Men held freedom dearer than life and partisans became patriots. The stain of political dishonor was cleansed with blood and a nation's life was dearer than one's own. Worcester had no humble part in this grand awakening, this beneficent fusion of the political with the moral forces.

The fight to end slavery nationally continued throughout the 1800s. After Missouri was admitted to the union in 1821 as a slave state, the debate began to grow more intense. Voices emerged in Worcester in 1838 when a convention of eighty ministers from throughout Worcester County led by Reverend George Allen met in Worcester to make a declaration against slavery. Two societies were formed that day, the North Division Anti-Slavery Society and the South Division Anti-Slavery Society. Lewis wrote, "Both societies were vigilant, persevering, sparing no party or sect which failed in duty to freedom, and ceased not from their work until the principles for which they were formed had been accepted by the country, and had become embodied in the National Constitution."

Several prominent voices emerged from this convention, but none were more important than Abby Kelley, later Abby Kelley Foster after she married another noted abolitionist, Stephen Symonds Foster. Kelley was born on January 15, 1811, in Pelham, Massachusetts, a town about fifty miles northwest of Worcester, but her family moved to Worcester in her infancy. According to the book *I Speak for My Slave Sister* by Margaret Hope Bacon, a lecture Kelley attended on slavery by William Lloyd Garrison, noted abolitionist and publisher of the foremost anti-slavery paper of the day, the *Liberator,* inspired her to take up the cause. She would later become a friend and confidante of Garrison.

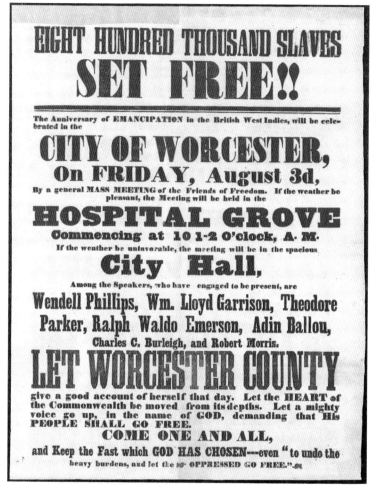

A poster for an antislavery meeting in Worcester with William Lloyd Garrison and Ralph Waldo Emerson among the speakers. *Boston Public Library, Rare Books Department.*

In 1836, Kelley got a teaching job in Lynn, Massachusetts, where she joined a women's anti-slavery society and soon got deeply involved in the movement. Through sources like the *Liberator* and her anti-slavery society, she got to know two sisters from South Carolina, Angelina and Sarah Grimke, both speakers against the ills of slavery. Through their correspondences with Kelley, the sisters encouraged her to see them speak at the inaugural Anti-Slavery Convention of American Women in New York City in May 1837. It was attended by women only, so the Grimkes and the other speakers addressed only a female audience. At that point in time, women rarely were permitted to lecture in front of men or a mixed audience that included men.

Kelley met not only the Grimke sisters at the convention, but other pioneering women who championed the cause, like Lucretia Mott and Maria Chapman, the latter of whom founded the convention. Kelley got directly involved in the group, joining a committee that drafted a call for women to join the anti-slavery movement. She returned home invigorated as she worked to further advocate against slavery. As she wrote to her sister Olive in 1837, her course was now set, as Bacon captured in her book.

> *I cannot tell you any news concerning myself. I pace the same old track, which is become so smooth there is neither side nor fall, but I enjoy a good degree of comfort, not withstanding. My variety is made up in watching the progress of moral enterprises. The temperance reform, embracing Grahamism and Abolition and Peace—and these three questions are sufficient to take up all spare time. Tis a great joy to see the world grow better in anything. Indeed, I think endeavors to improve mankind is the only subject worth living for.*

Fully involved now with the Anti-Slavery Convention of American Women, Kelley attended the second annual convention in Philadelphia as a member of the arrangements committee. The convention ran from May 15 to May 18 at Pennsylvania Hall, and the attendees included a mix of both men and women. Among the speakers were many of her idols, including Garrison, Angelina Grimke (who had married an architect named Theodore Weld) and Lucretia Mott. At the convention, Kelley became an active participant as a committee member. She even offered a resolution that, in effect, called for reparations to be paid to northern slaves. According to the proceedings, available from the Library of Congress:

> *Whereas, a vast portion of the wealth of the North has accrued, and is still accruing, from the slave system, either directly in the holding of slaves, by Northern citizens, or indirectly by our social and commercial intercourse with slaveholding communities; therefore, Resolved, That we are very deeply implicated in the sin of using our brother's service without wages, and of holding in our hands the gains of oppression; consequently it is our duty to bring forth fruits meet for repentance, by laboring devotedly in the service of the spoiled, and by contributing with unsparing liberality to the treasury of the slave.*

While the convention was going on, a mob of protesters had gathered outside Pennsylvania Hall, violently opposed to having the female abolitionists in their city. The protests grew louder and more unruly as the convention went on. While speakers were on stage, rocks were thrown through the windows. On Thursday night, after the third day of the convention, the mob set fire to the grand old Pennsylvania Hall, burning it to the ground. But the women would not be deterred, moving the proceedings to nearby Temperance Hall.

Abby Kelley Foster was a pioneer as one of the most forceful speakers in the country against slavery. *Schomburg Center for Research in Black Culture, Jean Blackwell Hutson Research and Reference Division, The New York Public Library. "Abby Kelley Foster." The New York Public Library Digital Collections.*

Angelina Grimke Weld told the audience: "That we have heard, with grief and shame, of the burning of Pennsylvania Hall, last evening, but rejoice in fulness of hope that God will overrule evil for good, by causing the flames which consumed that beautiful Hall, dedicated to virtue, liberty, and independence, to light up the fires of freedom on every hill-top and in every valley in the state of Pennsylvania, and our country at large."

The mob gathered outside Temperance Hall, too, and attempted to storm the meeting, but security personnel barred the doors to keep them out. According to the proceedings, "The Pennsylvania Hall having been burned by a mob, on Thursday evening, and much excitement still prevailing, the managers of Temperance Hall, fearing for the safety of their building, refused to open the doors."

The convention was notable because it marked the first time that Kelley spoke at an anti-slavery convention. During one of the lectures, she stood up, prompted by her friends, to address the mixed audience of men and women. She left quite an impression with her fiery words. As documented by the Archives of Women's Political Communication at Iowa State University, Kelley said:

> *The parable of Lazarus and the rich man we may well bring home to ourselves. The North is that rich man. How he is clothed in purple and fine linen, and fare sumptuously every day! Yonder, YONDER, at a little distance, is the gate where lies the Lazarus of the South, full of sores, and*

desiring to be fed with the crumbs that fall from our luxurious table. Look! see him there; even the dogs are more merciful than we. Oh! see him where he lies!! We have long, very long, passed by with averted eyes. Ought not we to raise him up; and is there one in this Hall who sees nothing for himself to do?

Moments after Kelley finished, one of the protesters tossed a rock through the window that landed near her on the stage. It punctuated what had been a rousing and controversial speech that drew ire and disapproval from some in the crowd. But many others were blown away by Kelley's words. Grimke's husband, Theodore Weld, approached Kelley after the speech and told her, according to Bacon, "You were tremendous. After this, you'll have to be an antislavery lecturer. Abby, if you don't, God will smite you."

The great writer and orator Frederick Douglass, a former slave from Maryland who escaped north to New Bedford, Massachusetts, where he lived before moving to Lynn and later settling in Rochester, New York, also praised the speech. "In token of my respect and gratitude to you, for having stood forth so nobly in defense of Woman and the Slave. Our hearts have been cheered and animated and strengthened by your presence," Douglass wrote to Kelley, according to the National Park Service.

Kelley returned home from the convention to Lynn more committed than ever to ending slavery and becoming a voice of change. Later that year, she quit her job as a teacher and returned home to Worcester to look after her ailing mother. But she was now on a new career path, as she explained in a letter to her mother, chronicled in *Sketches of Representative Women in New England*: "My way is clear now: a new light has broken on me. How true it is, as history records, that all great reforms have been carried forward by weak and despised means! The talent, the learning, the wealth, the Church, and the State, are pledged to the support of slavery. I will go out among the honest-hearted common people, into the highways and byways, and cry, 'Pity the poor slave!' if I can do nothing more."

That meeting in Philadelphia spawned one of the great voices of the era—not only against slavery but also for women's rights, as will be discussed later. When she moved back to Worcester, Kelley became active in various abolitionist groups. She became one of the first women to join the American Anti-Slavery Society, run by William Lloyd Garrison. She became the first woman appointed to the executive committee of the society. Kelley also joined the New England Anti-Slavery Society, where

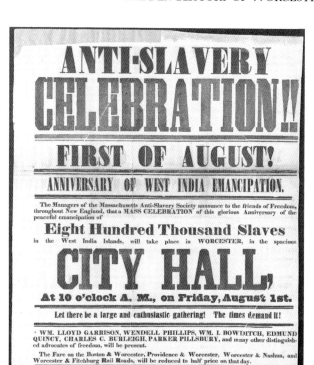

Left: A notice of an antislavery celebration held in Worcester. "Let there be a large and enthusiastic gathering! The times demand it!" *Boston Public Library, Rare Books Department.*

Below: A view of Worcester from Union Hill, circa 1840s. *Library of Congress Prints and Photographs Division.*

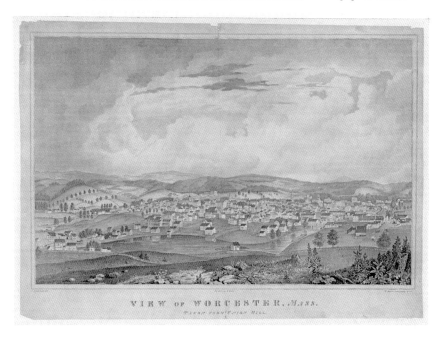

she was appointed to a committee—a first for that society. In her role, Kelley was charged with reaching out to churches to urge them to denounce slavery to their congregants.

"I am proud to be identified with the despised people of color," she wrote in a letter home, according to Bacon. "I thank the God of the poor that I was accounted worthy of such an honor."

Soon, Kelley was touring throughout Connecticut, Massachusetts, Rhode Island, New Hampshire, New York and elsewhere to speak out at churches and in other venues against slavery. She ruffled feathers wherever she went, not just with her fiery rhetoric but also because people were not used to being lectured to by a woman.

Between the two societies, Kelley was constantly on the road. While on the speaking circuit in New Hampshire, she met a kindred spirit in Stephen Symonds Foster, a young radical from Worcester who gained notoriety by interrupting church services to speak out against slavery. He usually had to be physically dragged out of the churches. Kelley and Foster had both gained reputations for their passionate views, but neither was deterred by the increasingly violent opposition that followed them on the trail.

Frederick Douglass, who was also touring the country speaking against slavery, became friends with Kelley and Foster, as their paths crisscrossed often. Douglass and Kelley spoke throughout the region, including at the lyceum in nearby Westminster, as Heywood noted. They also spoke at several venues in Worcester over the years, among them the famous Mechanics Hall, which opened in 1857 and is still open today. A portrait of Kelley hangs in the hall to this day, while one of Douglass soon will.

In his autobiography, *The Life and Times of Frederick Douglass*, Douglass discussed his relationship with Kelley and Foster.

I was much with Mr. Foster during the tour in Rhode Island, and though at times he seemed to me extravagant and needlessly offensive in his manner of presenting his ideas, yet take him for all in all, he was one of the most impressive advocates the cause of the American slave ever had. No white man ever made the black man's cause more completely his own. Abby Kelley, since Abby Kelley Foster, was perhaps the most successful of any of us. Her youth and simple Quaker beauty, combined with her wonderful earnestness, her large knowledge and great logical power, bore down all opposition in the end, wherever she spoke, though she was before pelted with foul eggs, and no less foul words from the noisy mobs which attended us.

Frederick Douglass, the great orator and former slave, said Kelley Foster "was perhaps the most successful of any of us." *National Portrait Gallery, Smithsonian Institution.*

After that initial meeting in New Hampshire, Foster and Kelley parted ways, but they would correspond frequently until they met again on speaking engagements in New York State. By this time, they had fallen in love. Before long, on December 21, 1845, they got married. They moved back to Worcester and moved into a large farmhouse they purchased in the western part of town at 116 Mower Street, which they called Liberty Farm. There, they had a daughter, Alla, in 1847.

Liberty Farm, now listed as a National Historic Landmark, became a stop on the Underground Railroad—a network of private safehouses where escaped slaves could stay on their way to freedom in the North. One of the first highly organized routes was established in 1842 by Reverend Charles Turner Torrey of Scituate, Massachusetts, who was arrested in 1844 for "stealing slaves."

Worcester, a popular stop on the Underground Railroad, was called the "lode-star" for fugitive slaves in the region, as William Siebert, author of the book *The Underground Railroad in Massachusetts*, detailed.

In the early 1830's, the Rev. Samuel J. May was living at Brooklyn and maintained an understanding with Effingham L. Capron at Uxbridge,

Massachusetts, to provide shelter and guidance for Underground passengers. Some of these evidently stopped first at East Douglass. In that case they received considerate treatment at the hands of Solomon P. Snow, who for a few years was the pastor of the Wesleyan Methodist Church there. One evening in 1849, while the Snow children were at home alone, a stalwart negro came to the house and frightened them badly. He was fleeing from pursuers, who had fired at him and wounded him in the hand. The parents returned soon, cared for and fed their visitor and sent him on to Uxbridge, which lies five miles to the east. From Uxbridge the distance to Worcester is sixteen miles, northwest. Being a strong anti-slavery community, Worcester was the lode-star for fugitive slaves in that region.

There was no map or guide on the network of stops; it was navigated by word of mouth to keep the stations secret from authorities. But there were several stops in Worcester, including Liberty Farm, where the Fosters lived. The Fosters built a five-by-ten-foot secret vault in their cellar, accessible by a trapdoor in the floor, where the runaway slaves would hide until they were free to move to the next stop. From the time they bought the aptly named Liberty Farm until the day slavery was abolished with the adoption of the Emancipation Proclamation in 1863, the Fosters helped thousands of slaves to their freedom. There are accounts of other stops in the city, as Siebert detailed.

A bewildered fugitive could find friends almost anywhere in the county. Too often, however, we do not know the names of the persons who made a practice of harboring slaves. Among the many Quakers of the city, we know only Edward Earle. The Hon. George F. Hoar was of the opinion that Charles Hadwen, another Quaker, who dwelt at some distance from any traveled road a little way out of Worcester, kept a refuge for the wayfarers. In 1847 Stephen Foster and his wife, Abby Kelly Foster, bought a farm at the foot of Paxton Hills in Tatnuck, a part of the suburbs of the city. There they lived for twenty-five years and sheltered fugitives until the outbreak of the Civil War, from which fact their place became known as "the Liberty Farm." The cellar of their house was divided by a brick wall, which was pierced by two doors. One of the halves of the cellar consisted of two rooms, in one of which was a closet at the side of which was a secret vault, five by ten feet in size. The only entrance to this vault was a trapdoor in the floor of the room above. It was in this vault that the Fosters usually secreted their negro guests.

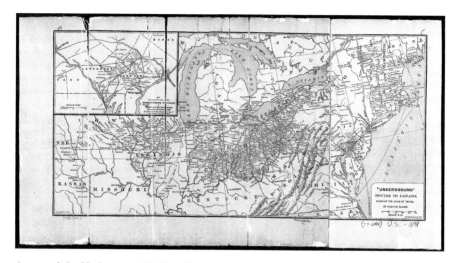

A map of the Underground Railroad, showing the routes slaves took to get to freedom. *Lionel Pincus and Princess Firyal Map Division, The New York Public Library. "Underground routes to Canada." The New York Public Library Digital Collections.*

When Thomas Wentworth Higginson settled in Worcester as the pastor of the Worcester Free Church near Harrington Corner, the church became a hub for local anti-slavery activities. Higginson had an Underground Railroad station there at the church and would drive the runaway slaves up to the next stop at Liberty Farm.

"In 1852 I removed to Worcester, into a strong anti-slavery community of which my 'Free Church' was an important factor. Fugitives came some times to the city, and I have driven them at midnight to the farm of the veteran Abolitionists, Stephen and Abby Kelley Foster, in the suburbs of the city," Higginson wrote in his book *Cheerful Yesterdays*.

From Liberty Farm, the Underground Railroad headed north through the towns of Westminster and Fitchburg. There were many "unseen highways" through these towns, as Deacon Joshua T. Everett of Westminster detailed in a letter published by the Danvers Historical Society in *Old Anti-Slavery Days*. "And in the north part of the county we constructed a number of unseen highways, over which the poor slave was helped on to Canada. Yes, fleeing to Canada to escape the infernal clutches of the slave-holder! I remember one very fine young woman about thirty years old, with her babe nearly a year old, brought to our depot in Everettville by an Abolition friend in the part of our county south of our depot."

As Siebert wrote, there was no map of the northern routes, but various accounts shed light on some of the stops. "Unfortunately, Mr. Everett has left no description or map of these routes. One of them evidently ran from Worcester twenty-one miles west of north to Westminster, whence the passengers could be transferred six miles northeastward to Fitchburg, or eight miles northwestward to North Ashburnham."

Noted folk and primitive-art painter and portrait artist Robert Peckham opened his home on Academy Street in Westminster as a stop on the Underground Railroad, his youngest daughter confirmed years later, according to the National Gallery of Art, which ran a retrospective of his work in 2013. It is also believed that the home of Ezra Wood was a stop on the route. Wood, who worked as a town assessor and selectman in Westminster and was a staunch abolitionist, lived on the corner of what is now Depot Road and Route 2A. The house, known as the Ezra Wood-Levi Warner House, still stands and is listed in the National Register of Historic Places.

"Not only did the apostles of the anti-slavery gospel find a welcome and a generous hearing here, but the panting fugitive, fleeing from the prison house of Southern bondage and the cruelties of an inhuman master or overseer, was granted temporary shelter and help on his way to Canada—then a refuge for the weary and oppressed," wrote William Sweetzer Heywood in his book *The History of Westminster, Massachusetts.*

Pastor Orlando White of Westminster also confirmed Westminster's prominent role, according to Heywood's town history. "Those were years of intense excitement on the great questions of Slavery, Temperance, and the Oberlin Theology. The Fugitive Slave Law was just beginning to be executed and this town was one of the stations of the 'underground rail road.'"

In her account, *Antislavery Reminscences,* Elizabeth Buffum Chace, an abolitionist from Providence, explained the process the fugitive slaves went through and the path they took to safety in Canada.

Slaves in Virginia would secure passage, either secretly or with consent of the Captains, in small trading vessels at Norfolk or Portsmouth, and thus be brought into some port in New England, where their fate depended on the circumstances into which they happened to fall. A few, landing in some town on Cape Cod, would reach New Bedford, and thence be sent by an abolitionist there to Fall River, to be sheltered by Nathaniel B. Borden and his wife, who was my sister Sarah, and sent by them to Valley Falls in the darkness of night, and in a closed carriage, with Robert Adams, a most faithful on the Providence and Worcester railroad, acquaint the conductor with the facts, enlist his interest in their behalf, and then leave them in his care, to be transferred at Worcester, to the

Vermont road, from which, by a previous general arrangement, they were received by a Unitarian clergyman named Young, and sent by him to Canada, where they uniformly arrived safely.

To determine the impact of these efforts, Reverend Hiram K. Wilson traveled to Ontario, Canada, as a missionary in the winter of 1856 to determine how many former slaves had made it to freedom, according to Siebert. Wilson counted about thirty-five thousand freed slaves; by 1860, the number had climbed to at least forty-five thousand, which Wilson suspected was probably a low estimate. Many other freed slaves entered Canada through Detroit, Niagara Falls and Ogdensburg, New York, while the hundreds who traveled through New England settled at Stanstead, St. John's and Montreal. Others escaped through the Maritime Provinces to England. The actions of these freedom fighters not only saved lives but also preserved generations of families.

6

Abe Lincoln in Worcester
and the Free Soil Movement

The issue of slavery was front and center in the presidential election of
1848, which pitted Whig Zachary Taylor, a major general who was
a hero of the Mexican-American War, and Democrat Lewis Cass.
While Taylor, a southerner from Virginia, did not promote the expansion
of slavery to the new western territories that were annexed after the war, he
did own a plantation and slaves. Politically, Taylor was more interested in
preserving the union and keeping the status quo than speaking out forcefully
one way or the other about slavery. Cass, on the other hand, fully supported
the "Doctrine of Popular Sovereignty," which stated that the people of each
state or territory annexed after the Mexican-American War should decide
for themselves if they want to be a slaveholding state. This was not a popular
stance in Worcester, as the region was predominantly anti-slavery. The city
would, once again, play a major role in shaping national politics.

The political winds began to shift in June 1848 after the Whig National
Convention in Philadelphia. Charles Allen of Worcester, who had served
in the Massachusetts State Senate and House, attended as a Whig delegate
from Massachusetts. He returned home deeply frustrated that the party's
platform had failed to fully commit to denouncing the expansion of
slavery to the western territories. Allen and his compatriots were then
known as "Conscience Whigs" for their views on ending slavery, while
the Taylor wing of the party was known as "Cotton Whigs," because they
were more ambivalent toward ending slavery and were more interested
in their cotton plantations.

"You have put one ounce too much on the strong back of Northern endurance, you have even presumed that the State which led on the first revolution for liberty will now desert that cause for the miserable boon of the Vice-Presidency. Sir, Massachusetts will spurn the bribe. We declare the Whig party of the Union this day dissolved," Allen said, according to J.W. Lewis's *History of Worcester, Massachusetts.*

His mention of the "bribe" of the vice presidency referred to Massachusetts congressman Abbott Lawrence, who was being considered as Taylor's running mate, narrowly losing out to Millard Fillmore. "I express for myself what I believe to be the sentiments of that State (Mass.) and I say that we cannot consent that this shall go forth as the unanimous voice of this convention. The Whig party of the North are not to be allowed to nominate their statesman. We declare the Whig party of the Union this day dissolved," Allen said at the convention, according to Nutt's *The History of Worcester and Its People.*

Allen returned home to Worcester and immediately got to work organizing local opposition to the Whigs, with the help of the *Massachusetts Spy*, which had been so influential during the American Revolution. Now the *Spy*, being run by John Milton Earle, was a major force in the cause to end slavery. It published a call to political arms in the June 21, 1848 edition, two weeks after the Whig Convention, according to Nutt. "The citizens of Worcester and vicinity, opposed to the nomination of Taylor and Cass, are invited to meet at City Hall, Wednesday evening, June 21st, at 7:30, and make arrangements for the approaching convention to be held the 28th. Hon. Charles Allen, a delegate to the late Philadelphia convention, has been invited, and has consented to address the convention. All friends of the proposed movement from neighboring towns are cordially invited to be present."

On June 28, some 5,000 people attended what was initially called the People's Convention of Massachusetts at the Old City Hall, the main meeting hall of the day, located at the time near Main and Front Streets. The convention was organized by Allen, along with local merchant Henry Chamberlain, William A. Wallace of the *Spy*, Oliver Harrington, George Russell, Edward Southwick, Joseph Boyden and local blacksmith Albert Tolman. (Tolman, incidentally, is credited by some sources with inventing a form of the rickshaw in 1848. Tolman's "man-drawn lorry" was built for a missionary traveling in South America.)

William W. Rice, a teacher at Leicester Academy and later mayor of Worcester, detailed how the convention led to the birth of a new political party, the Free Soil Party, as Nutt outlined in his book. It was a movement driven by the people, as opposed to the political class or the elite.

"The great men of the city, were not there, nor in sympathy with it," W.W. Rice wrote, as Nutt chronicled in his book.

The press had not advocated it. The clergymen were cold. The merchants and professional men passed it by. But the men from the shops, who were really rulers of the city then, as they have been ever since, were there to express their sovereign will. They realized the importance of the crisis, and, disregarding the wishes and advice of those to whom they had been accustomed to trust the management of their political interests, they had resolved to take matters into their own hands and had come out to do their work themselves.... That night witnessed the birth of the Free Soil Party, which sprang full armed from the brain and will of Charles Allen, ready to do battle against Whigs, Democrats and all other opponents.

The meeting featured some prominent speakers, including Concord politician and lawyer Samuel Hoar, future Massachusetts senator Charles Sumner, future Massachusetts senator and vice president Henry Wilson and Ohio congressman Joshua Giddings. But it was Allen, the man who started it all, who stole the show. Rice, who was also in attendance, provided an account of his speech, as documented by Nutt.

It occupied nearly two hours in its delivery. In style it is a masterpiece. In its adaptation to the occasion of its delivery, in its power to produce the results desired by the speaker, it was scarcely, if ever, surpassed or equaled....He referred to the resolutions of that convention as charging him to "vote for a candidate for President who should be in favor of preserving the territories of the United States free from the stain of Slavery....We reject Gen. Taylor throughout the North and throughout the Free States."

Allen was greeted with "deafening" shouts of approval from the assembled.

Perhaps most important, the attendees at the convention passed a resolution that would alter the course of American history. "Resolved, That Massachusetts wears no chains and spurns all bribes; that Massachusetts goes now and will ever go for free soil and free men, for free lips and a free press, for a free land and a free world."

In Massachusetts, it marked the birth of the short-lived but influential Free Soil Party, which had the sole mission of ending slavery. "They have spoken a voice not to be mistaken and taken a stand never to be receded from till the last battle is fought and the victory won for Liberty and Right," the *Spy* wrote after the convention, according to Lewis.

The Free Soil Party was a conglomeration of several smaller parties. In New York State, a faction of Democrats known as the Barnburners was emerging, upset by the nomination of Cass. Like the Conscience Whigs turned Free Soilers, the Barnburners held their own convention on June 22, 1848, in Upstate New York to nominate former president Martin Van Buren to run against Taylor and Cass in the upcoming election. There was also opposition to Taylor from the Liberty Party, which formed in 1840 on the platform of opposing slavery. The Liberty Party had run James Birney of Kentucky for president in 1840 and 1844, losing both times. This melting pot of anti-slavery reformers made up of Conscience Whigs, Barnburners and the Liberty Party coalesced in the summer of 1848 as the Free Soil Party, which Charles Allen was a major part of organizing.

The first Free Soil Party Convention was held in August 1848 in Buffalo, New York, to officially nominate a candidate for president. Van Buren, from Kinderhook, New York, was a former Democrat who served as the ninth president of the U.S. He was upset with his party's nomination of Cass not only for his views on the expansion of slavery, but also because Van Buren blamed Cass for tanking his nomination for reelection in 1844. The Liberty Party had nominated Senator John Hale of New Hampshire, while the Free Soilers put up Ohio representative Joshua Giddings and Charles Francis Adams, the son of President John Quincy Adams and the grandson of President John Adams. Van Buren, who had by far the greatest name recognition, was picked as the candidate to run for the Free Soil Party in 1848, with Adams as his running mate. In a span of just two months, the Free Soil Party had become a major player in national politics.

The emergence of the Free Soil Party, with a former president as its standard-bearer, sent shockwaves throughout the political world. It caught the attention of a young Republican congressman from Illinois named Abraham Lincoln, who was an anti-slavery Whig. But, as a party man, Lincoln was supporting the Whig candidate, Taylor. Lincoln, a rising political star, had been elected to the House just a year before, in 1847. He became close friends with his fellow congressman who represented Worcester County, Charles Hudson of Westminster, who was also a Whig.

Hudson was one of Lincoln's closest friends and confidantes. He later wrote a book about Lincoln, *The Character of Abraham Lincoln*, and several of his personal letters to Lincoln are published in the Library of Congress as part of the Lincoln Papers. Later, Hudson served as the assessor of internal revenue when Lincoln became president. Hudson was not in any way for slavery, but he, like Lincoln, was loyal to the party and its nominee.

In a memoriam written about Hudson in 1881, Henry Smith wrote: "He was in the House with Lincoln and (Stephen) Douglas, and more than once grappled in debate with the latter. With Abraham Lincoln, his friendship was warm and for a lifetime; and Slavery had no better haters than such representative Whigs as these. They remained good Whigs when they became Republicans, and were forecasted Republicans while they were yet Whigs."

Hudson was not in agreement with Allen's declaration that the Whig Party had dissolved in Massachusetts. He was breathing proof that it was alive, if not well. However, the fact remained, as Lincoln biographer Albert Beveridge wrote, "Thousands of Whigs were flocking to the new Free Soil party. The younger Whigs were especially militant in opposition to the old and moribund organization."

Looking to shore up support for the Whigs in Massachusetts in a state that had become a Free Soil stronghold, Hudson invited Lincoln to attend the Massachusetts State Whig Convention on September 13, 1848, in Worcester and speak before a gathering of Whigs the night before at Old City Hall in Worcester, according to Arthur Prentice Rugg's *Abraham Lincoln in Worcester*.

The tall, rangy Lincoln had gained a reputation as a "ready and forceful speaker," said Rugg. Hudson, perhaps recognizing Lincoln's ability to persuade a crowd, likely saw him as someone to fortify support for the Whigs and mend fences with the Free Soilers. Lincoln and Hudson believed that a vote for Van Buren and the Free Soil Party would be at the expense of Taylor and, in essence, equal a vote for Cass. That would be the worst-case scenario, as Cass was supportive of the western territories deciding for themselves on slavery, while Taylor was not.

Lincoln arrived in Worcester around September 12, a day before the Whig Convention, at the invitation of Hudson. He stayed at the Worcester House, a hotel that used to be the home of the newly elected mayor of Worcester, Levi Lincoln Jr., on the corner of Main and Elm Streets. The Worcester House was a Greek revival home that had been converted to a hotel in 1834 after Lincoln moved down the street to his new mansion at 49 Elm Street.

Alexander Bullock, the chair of the local Whig Party committee, had arranged for a public meeting of Whigs the night before the convention at City Hall. He had asked "several men of prominence to speak at the City Hall gathering," according to Beveridge, but several did not accept the invitation.

Old City Hall in Worcester, where Abraham Lincoln spoke on September 12, 1848, to local Whig leaders. *The Miriam and Ira D. Wallach Division of Art, Prints and Photographs: Photography Collection, The New York Public Library. "City Hall." The New York Public Library Digital Collections.*

"But as the sun was descending, I was told that Abraham Lincoln, member of Congress from Illinois, was stopping at one of the hotels in town. I had heard of him before, and at once called upon him and made known my wish that he would address the meeting of the evening, to which he readily assented," Bullock said, according to Rugg.

But before the speech at City Hall, Abraham Lincoln was invited to attend a dinner at the current home of Mayor Lincoln on 49 Elm Street. Mayor Lincoln was the son of Levi Lincoln Sr., the former governor. Like his father, Mayor Lincoln spent his life in public service. Levi Lincoln Jr. served in the Massachusetts legislature from 1812 to 1823 and then was elected governor in 1825. Lincoln held the state's highest office until 1834, when he stepped down to run for Congress in 1834 to fill the seat vacated by John Davis, who succeeded Lincoln as governor. Lincoln served in the U.S. House of Representatives until 1841.

Lincoln's gorgeous mansion, which featured stately pillars and spacious grounds, was built in 1835, the year after his term as governor ended. In his biography of Abraham Lincoln, Beveridge cited Abraham Lincoln's own recollection of the event at the Mayor Levi Lincoln mansion.

"I had been chosen to Congress then from the Wild West," he is reported to have recounted, "and with hayseed in my hair I went to Massachusetts, the most cultured State in the Union, to take a few lessons in deportment. That was a grand dinner—a superb dinner; by far the finest I ever saw in my life. And the great men who were there too! Why I can tell you just how they were arranged at table."

Henry Gardner, a future Massachusetts governor, was also in attendance at the dinner. In *Herndon's Life of Lincoln*, by William Herndon, Gardner said that Lincoln "remarked upon the beauty of the china, the fineness of the silverware and the richness of all the table appointments and spoke of the company of distinguished and thoroughly educated men whom he met there in the animated, free and intimate conversation inspired by such an accomplished host as Governor Lincoln." Gardner also recalled Abraham and his host Levi joking about their identical last name. "I well remember the jokes between Governor Lincoln and Abraham Lincoln as to their presumed relationship. At last, the latter said: 'I hope we both belong, as the Scotch say, to the same clan; but I know one thing, and that is, that we are both good Whigs.'"

Later that night, Lincoln spoke at City Hall. According to Herndon, Gardner, who was also in attendance for that address, said the future president brought down the house.

> No one there had ever heard him on the stump, and in fact knew anything about him. When he was announced, his tall, angular, bent form, and his manifest awkwardness and low tone of voice, promised nothing interesting. But he soon warmed to his work. His style and manner of speaking were novelties in the East. He repeated anecdotes, told stories admirable in humor and in point, interspersed with bursts of true eloquence, which constantly brought down the house. His sarcasm of Cass, Van Buren and the Democratic party was inimitable, and whenever he attempted to stop, the shouts of "Go on! go on!" were deafening. He probably spoke over an hour, but so great was the enthusiasm time could not be measured. It was doubtless one of the best efforts of his life.

There was little coverage of Lincoln's pre-convention speech at City Hall in the Worcester papers, perhaps due to the fact that Worcester was a Free Soil town.

"For sound, conclusive reasoning and ready wit it is unsurpassed in the campaign. It was listened to by the crowded audience with an untiring interest, applauded during its delivery, and enthusiastically cheered at its close," the *National Aegis* wrote. The account, according to Beveridge, said that Lincoln "was greatly liked" and that his "was a style new to our people, and there was a general call for him as a speaker."

The *Spy*, which supported the Free Soil Party, provided some color on the proceedings but offered little on Lincoln, according to Beveridge. In fact, the *Spy* erroneously referred to him as "Mr. Abraham Lincoln, the recently defeated Taylor candidate in the 7th Illinois district in Illinois for re-election to Congress." The paper had to later print a correction, as Lincoln was not a defeated candidate; rather, he had declined to run for a second term. But the retraction was not without a further dig at Lincoln. "The organ (referring to the True Whig) complains of our suggestion that Abraham Lincoln was a defeated candidate. We knew that a Cass man had been elected in his district, and hence inferred erroneously it appears that Mr. Lincoln was the defeated candidate. It turns out, however, that it was another Taylor candidate who was defeated, Mr. Lincoln foreseeing the danger having prudently withdrawn himself."

The *Boston Daily Advertiser* published a more detailed account of Lincoln's address, as printed in *The Works of Abraham Lincoln, Volume 2*.

> *Mr. Kellogg then introduced to the meeting the Hon. Abraham Lincoln, Whig member of Congress from Illinois, a representative of Free Soil. Mr. Lincoln has a very tall and thin figure, with an intellectual face, showing a searching mind, and a cool judgment. He spoke in a clear and cool, and very eloquent manner, for an hour and a half, carrying the audience with him in his able arguments and brilliant illustrations—only interrupted by warm and frequent applause....He then began to show the fallacy of some of the arguments against Gen. Taylor, making his chief theme the fashionable statement of all those who oppose him, (the old Locofocos as well as the new) that he has no principles, and that the Whig party have abandoned their principles by adopting him as their candidate. He maintained that Gen. Taylor occupied a high and unexceptionable Whig ground, and took for his first instance and proof of this his statement in the Allison letter— with regard to the Bank, Tariff, Rivers and Harbors, etc.—that the will of the people should produce its own results, without Executive influence.*

The Allison letters were two letters that Taylor wrote to his brother-in-law Captain J.S. Allison before the election, both printed in newspapers. The letters outlined Taylor's views on the presidency and key issues and declared that he would not be a partisan president but one who represented all the people. The letters were viewed as critical to Taylor's electoral win that year. Lincoln told the crowd in Worcester that his candidate, Taylor, was more interested in serving the will of the people than kowtowing to the party line. According to the *Advertiser*'s report, Lincoln said: "The Whigs here maintained for years that neither the influence, the duress, or the prohibition of the Executive should control the legitimately expressed will of the people, and now that on that very ground, Gen. Taylor says that he should use the power given him by the people to do, to the best of his judgment, the will of the people, he is accused of want of principle, and of inconsistency in position."

On slavery, Lincoln said he, along with the people of Illinois, agreed entirely with the people of Massachusetts on this subject, "except perhaps that they did not keep so constantly thinking about it." In other words, people from Massachusetts were far more passionately opposed to slavery than his constituents.

> *But the question of the extension of slavery to new territories of this country is a part of our responsibility and care and is under our control. In opposition to this Mr. Lincoln believed that the self-named "Free Soil" party was far behind the Whigs. Both parties opposed the extension. As he understood it, the new party had no principle except this opposition. If their platform held any other, it was in such a general way that it was like the pair of pantaloons the Yankee peddler offered for sale, "large enough for any man, small enough for any boy."*

If the Free Soil and Whig vote were split and the result was the election of Cass, "plans of farther extension of territory would be encouraged, and those of the extension of slavery would meet no check," said Lincoln. The *Advertiser* article concluded that Lincoln, who was wearing a long linen duster, received a rousing ovation. "At the close of this truly masterly and convincing speech, the audience gave three enthusiastic cheers for Illinois, and three more cheers for the eloquent Whig member from that State."

The next morning, September 13, Lincoln and several others spoke briefly to a crowd of delegates and citizens near the railway station in Worcester, according to Beveridge. Later that day, he attended the Whig Convention, where speakers included his friend Hudson, along with local Whig leaders like Congressman Robert Winthrop, former U.S. senator Rufus Choate and Daniel Webster. Lincoln did not speak at the convention but was described by Beveridge as a "silent listener."

A few days after the Whig Convention, Lincoln went to Boston, where he addressed an audience on September 22 near Faneuil Hall. But it was another presenter that day who enthralled Lincoln: former New York governor William Seward. Beveridge called Seward "the most promising of the rising statesmen of the day." He had come to Massachusetts because of the "bold declarations in the Whig platform adopted at Worcester." It was Seward's forceful rhetoric on slavery, where he said it would be eradicated in his lifetime, that really resonated with Lincoln.

"But the dominant note of Seward's speech was resistance to slavery and to the South. The time would come, he said, and that, too, in his day, 'when the free people would free the slaves in this country.' This is to be accomplished by moral force, without injustice…by paying a full remuneration for so great a blessing," Beveridge wrote of Seward's speech. "Of the Whig and Democratic parties, one had its foundations in South Carolina, the other on the Rock of Plymouth. If the third party should 'draw off all the advocates of Liberty, we shall have left the two great parties, ready to bow before the aristocracy of the South.'"

After the speech, Lincoln approached Seward, who, incidentally, Lincoln would later appoint as his secretary of state when he was president. "I have been thinking about what you said in your speech. I reckon you are right. We have got to deal with this slavery question and got to give much more attention to it hereafter than we have been doing," according to Ida Tarbell, author of the article "The Life of Lincoln."

The trip to Worcester proved to be a turning point for Lincoln on slavery. It was on this sojourn to Massachusetts that he realized the depth of the opposition to slavery in this region and the unwavering commitment to defeat it. Tarbell said that Lincoln

> won something in New England of vastly deeper importance than a reputation for making popular campaign speeches. Here for the first time, he caught a glimpse of the utter impossibility of ever reconciling, the northern conviction that slavery was evil and unendurable and the southern claim that it was divine and necessary; and he began here to realize that something must be done. He experienced for the first time the full meaning of the "free soil" sentiment as the new abolition sentiment was called.

When he returned to Washington, D.C., in December of that year for the second session of the Thirtieth Congress, Lincoln had fully resolved to do something regarding slavery, wrote Tarbell.

Taylor wound up winning the state of Massachusetts with 45 percent of the vote, followed by Van Buren at 28 percent and Cass at 26 percent. Taylor, of course, went on to be the twelfth president of the United States on November 7, 1848. But the story doesn't end there for the Free Soil pioneers from Worcester. The next March, Charles Allen, the Worcester man who helped spark the Free Soil revolution, won a seat in Congress, defeating the Whig Hudson from Westminster, who had served for four terms.

Allen has the distinction of being one of only a few Free Soilers to ever serve in Congress, because, by 1854, the party would be gone. So would the Whigs. The catalyst was the passage of the Kansas-Nebraska Act in May

1854, which created those territories—later, states—and, more importantly, gave them popular sovereignty, which meant they could decide for themselves to be slave states. This led to increased tensions and raids to save slaves, an era that became known as "Bleeding Kansas." The two parties, along with anti-slavery Democrats, were so angered by this development that it made them realize that they had to come together to defeat slavery—or they would just split the vote. So, both parties dissolved and emerged as a new united entity, the Republican Party.

The Republican Party officially formed in 1854 in Ripon, Wisconsin, but Worcester was not far behind in embracing the new party. On July 20, 1854, at the "People's Convention" in Worcester, the Republican Party in Worcester officially formed. Among those in attendance were P. Emory Aldrich and P.W. Taft, both of Worcester, who were on the committee of resolution. According to Frank Abial Flower's *History of the Republican Party*, about twenty-five hundred people were in attendance, where the following resolution was approved: "Resolved, That in co-operation with the friends of freedom in other States we hereby form ourselves into the Republican Party of Massachusetts, pledged to the accomplishment of the following purposes, among which were the repeal of the Fugitive Slave Law, the restoration of liberty to Kansas and Nebraska, prohibition of slavery in all the territories, refusal of admission of any more slave states into the Union." According to Flower, among those in attendance were Charles Francis Adams, Henry Wilson, future Massachusetts senator George Frisbie Hoar and Ralph Waldo Emerson.

In just six short years, the Free Soil Party had a major impact on politics and policy in the United States. It not only pushed the Whigs to more forcefully oppose slavery, but it also served as the issue at the heart and soul of the new Republican Party, with Lincoln as its standard-bearer. The Free Soilers' single mission of free men on free soil and ending slavery became central to Lincoln's winning platform in 1860. And the seeds were planted in Worcester, as U.S. senator George Frisbie Hoar of Worcester so eloquently stated at the 200th anniversary of the naming of Worcester on October 14, 1884.

I claim for the people of Worcester city and county a service and leadership in the political revolution which achieved the freedom of the slave, to which the contribution of no individual is to be compared. Charles Allen did a heroic act, when, at Philadelphia, he predicted the dissolution of his party, then in the very delirium of anticipated triumph, and came

Senator George Frisbie Hoar called Worcester the birthplace of the antislavery cause. *Library of Congress Prints and Photographs Division.*

home to summon the people of his young city to his side. He was one of the very greatest of men. But he could scarcely have looked his neighbors in the face, had he done otherwise. Elsewhere, it was, at best, a party, that was on the side of freedom. Here, it was a people. I see that other localities are now making claim to be the birthplace of the Anti-slavery cause, which would hardly have acknowledged the paternity at the time. So, we will not discuss their title. But as surely as Faneuil Hall was the cradle of American Independence, so surely was Worcester the cradle of the later revolution.

Hoar had a long and distinguished career, first as an abolitionist and then as a member of the Massachusetts House and Senate. In 1869, he was elected to the U.S. House of Representatives, representing Worcester. He served two terms and then was elected to the U.S. Senate in 1877. He was one of the longest-serving senators of his day, elected to five terms, serving from 1877 until 1904, when he died while in office at the age of seventy-eight. He is buried at Sleepy Hollow Cemetery in Concord, Massachusetts, where he was born, but his legacy lives on in Worcester, where a statue of him stands for eternity outside City Hall.

7

Pastor Higginson and
the Raid on Boston

The worst fears of the Free Soilers came to fruition following the election of Zachary Taylor in 1848. Taylor died just sixteen months into his term of a stomach disease and was replaced by his vice president, Millard Fillmore. The Free Soilers were concerned that Taylor wasn't staunch enough in his denunciation of slavery, but now with Fillmore in office, they were extremely worried, as Fillmore was less of an ally than Taylor. In fact, shortly after taking office, Fillmore signed the controversial Fugitive Slave Act into law in 1850 as part of the Compromise of 1850. The Fugitive Slave Act required that all slaves who escaped to the North had to be returned to their masters if they were caught. Abolitionists called it the "Bloodhound Law," referring to the fact that dogs were sometimes used to track the escaped slaves. The law mandated that public officials and citizens of the Free States comply with the law.

While Fillmore saw this as a compromise to appease southern slaveholders, it only incensed the northern Whigs and Free Soilers. In Worcester, leading abolitionists met at City Hall in Worcester in both 1849 and 1851 to celebrate the anniversary of the emancipation of eight hundred thousand slaves in the British West Indies. "Let there be a large and enthusiastic gathering. The Times demand it!" a poster read. The event was put on by the Massachusetts Anti-Slavery Society. Among the speakers were Wendell Phillips, William Lloyd Garrison, Theodore Parker, Ralph Waldo Emerson, Adin Ballou, Charles Burleigh, Robert Morris, William Bowditch, Edmund Quincy and Parker Pillsbury. "Come at the call of three millions [sic] of our countrymen in slavery."

The Fugitive Slave Act ratcheted up the tension between the government and its citizens, particularly those in the Free States, who were bound by law to turn on these escaped slaves. The Underground Railroad became fraught with even more danger, as runaway slaves were subject to be returned to a life of slavery and those helping them escape would face steep fines. But for the Fosters and other abolitionists, it steeled their resolve. "We must all be ready to sacrifice our lives, and make this sacrifice today, if need be, for the cause of freedom," Abby Kelley Foster said, as quoted in Bacon's book. "No fugitive slave shall be taken from this city if throwing my body on the path of the kidnappers, and sacrificing my life, can prevent it."

There were many occurrences throughout the Free States in which abolitionists attempted to rescue and free fugitives who had been caught. There was a particularly dramatic rescue attempt of a fugitive slave named Anthony Burns that involved a pastor from Worcester named Thomas Wentworth Higginson. Burns had escaped enslavement from Colonel Charles Suttle in Richmond, Virginia, and made his way north to Boston through the Underground Railroad.

As a free man in Boston, Burns found work at a pie shop and a clothing store until May 24, 1854, when he was arrested for allegedly breaking into a jewelry store. Burns didn't actually rob the store—it was simply pretense to extradite him back to Suttle under the Fugitive Slave Act of 1850. However, Burns's lawyers were able to prove that the arrest was illegal, so the court proceedings were postponed for a few days while Burns was being held in a Boston jail by the U.S. marshal.

Upon word of Burns's arrest, the Vigilance Committee, a Boston-area group of abolitionists who formed to protect free Blacks from slave hunters or kidnappers, called a meeting for May 26, 1854. Higginson, the pastor of the Free Church of Worcester and an ardent abolitionist, attended a meeting of the committee at Faneuil Hall to develop a plan to break Burns free. There were sixty members in attendance, including Theodore Parker and Samuel Gridley Howe, two men who would later join Higginson as one of John Brown's Secret Six, along with Wendell Phillips and George Russell. The executive committee developed a plan to free Burns, as detailed by John McCymer and a team of researchers at Assumption College: "Resolved, That the perfidious seizure of Anthony Burns, in this city, on Wednesday evening last, on the lying pretence of having committed a crime against the laws of this State—his imprisonment as an alleged fugitive slave in the Court House, under guard of certain slave-catching

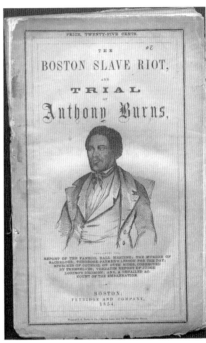

Left: Thomas Wentworth Higginson—pastor, abolitionist, writer and one of John Brown's "Secret Six"—was arrested in the raid to free former slave Anthony Burns. *Library of Congress Prints and Photographs Division.*

Right: The cover of a publication about the "Boston Slave Riot" and the Anthony Burns trial. *Photograph retrieved from the Library of Congress.*

ruffians—and his complicated trial as a piece of property to-morrow morning—are outrages never to be sanctioned or tamely submitted to."

That evening, after that meeting, the committee was able to rally hundreds of abolitionists to protest in front of the courthouse. But the rally soon turned violent as the protesters attempted to break down the courthouse door with a battering ram. Shots were fired, and a melee broke out. An account in the *Spy* detailed the event, which involved the killing of a U.S. marshal. It is quoted here, courtesy of Assumption College.

> *Entering upon the Eastern Avenue, in the space of a minute or two, several hundred people had collected, and the officers in the building closed the doors. Presently there was a rush to the West side, and a crowd of several hundred persons was assembled upon the opposite sidewalk. Several heads appeared from the windows in the third story, from one of which two pistols were*

discharged in quick succession. This seemed to exasperate the crowd most intensely, and a rush was made to the door. Finding that it would not yield readily, a piece of joist about ten feet long, seven inches wide, and two inches thick, was procured, and with it some six or eight strong men, soon battered down the door. The menials of the kidnapper, inside, all armed to the teeth, made a desperate resistance in the entry way, with clubs and cutlasses, and, just at this juncture, a dozen policemen from the Centre Watch House, arrived upon the ground, and, in a few moments arrested several persons, and took them to the Watch House. While thus engaged, several pistol shots were heard in the entry, by those outside, one of which, it was afterwards ascertained, had resulted in the death of one of the hired assassins of Liberty, in the employ of the kidnappers, named James Batchelder.

Soon, two companies of marines and two companies of artillery troops arrived on the scene. The police arrested several of the protesters, including Higginson and Martin Stowell of Worcester, a member of Higginson's church. There was some confusion over who killed the marshal, James Batchelder. As the *Spy* reported, per the Assumption College researchers, it was likely an accident. The article stated: "There is every reason to believe that Batchelder fell by the demonstration made upon the door, and there can be little doubt, that in the darkness, confusion, and terror, that prevailed inside at the time, he received the fatal shot from one of the bungling assistants of the Marshal, who report says, had been supplied with an abundance of Dutch courage from a neighboring restorator."

There were no charges for the murder, but seven men were indicted by the grand jury for forcibly obstructing the marshal in executing the warrant against Burns, according to Siebert's *The Underground Railroad in Massachusetts*. The seven men arrested included Parker, Higginson, Phillips, Stowell, John Cluer, John Morrison and Samuel Proudman. The men all posted bond, but their scheduled appearances in court on March 1, 1855, never happened, as the indictments were "quashed as being imperfect." Burns was not as fortunate. He lost his case in court and was extradited back to Suttle in Virginia. But approximately a year later, Burns was purchased by a group of wealthy Bostonians and set free. As a free man once again, Burns enrolled at Oberlin College in Ohio and then went on to become a Baptist preacher in Ontario, Canada.

Higginson, just one day after the attempted raid to free Burns, addressed his frustrations in his sermon, called "Massachusetts in Mourning." In it, he bemoaned another loss in the fight against slavery.

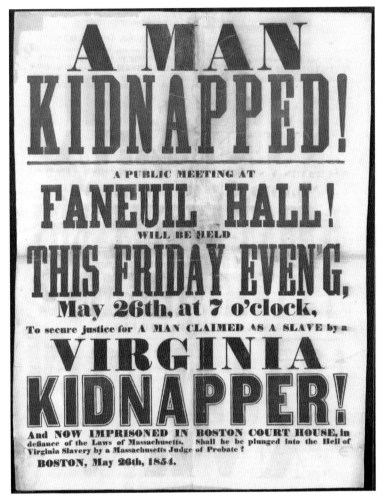

A poster promoting a meeting at Faneuil Hall seeking justice for Anthony Burns, who was taken "by a Virginia kidnapper" under the Fugitive Slave Act. *Boston Public Library, Rare Books Department.*

We talk of the Anti-Slavery sentiment as being stronger; but in spite of your Free Soil votes, your Uncle Tom's Cabin, and your New York Tribunes, here is the simple fact: the South beats us more and more easily every time.... No wonder that this excitement is turning Whigs and Democrats into Free Soilers, and Free Soilers into disunionists.....Name, if you can, a victory of Freedom, or a defeat of the Slave Power, within twenty years, except on the right of petition, and even that was only a recovery of lost ground.

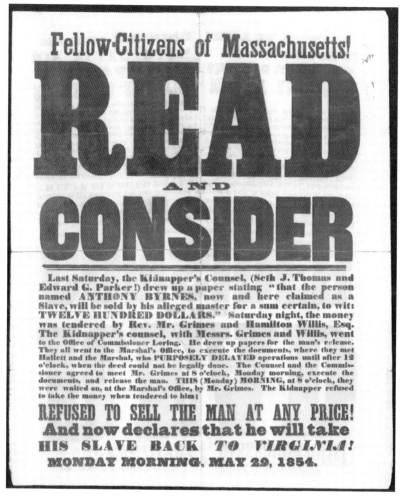

A poster informing the public about an attempt to secure the release of Anthony Burns before he was sent back to Virginia into slavery. *Boston Public Library, Rare Books Department.*

Higginson made a startling call to arms to the people of Worcester to stand up for the slaves and protect the free soil of Worcester.

If you think Worcester County is free, say so and act accordingly. Call a County Convention, and declare that you leave legal quibbles to lawyers, and parties to politicians, and plant yourselves on the simple truth that God never made a Slave, and that man shall neither make nor take one here! Over your own city, at least, you have power; but will you stand the test

*when it comes? Then do not try to avoid it. For one thing only I blush—
that a Fugitive has ever fled from here to Canada. Let it not happen again,
I charge you, if you are what you think you are. No longer conceal Fugitives
and help them on but show them and defend them. Let the Underground
Railroad stop here! Say to the South that Worcester, though a part of a
Republic, shall be as free as if ruled by a Queen! Hear, O Richmond! and
give ear, O Carolina! henceforth Worcester is Canada to the Slave! And
what will Worcester be to the kidnapper? I dare not tell; and I fear that
the poor sinner himself, if once recognized in our streets, would scarcely get
back to tell the tale.*

The question Higginson posed—"What will Worcester be to the kidnapper?"—was answered just a few months later, in October 1854, when a notorious "slave kidnapper" named Asa Butman arrived in town. Butman was the man who had kidnapped, or turned in, Burns as well as two other escaped slaves, Shadrach Minkins and Thomas Sims, in Boston. Butman was said to have been in Worcester investigating the role that Higginson played in the Burns rescue attempt and seeking witnesses for the impending trial of Higginson. Many abolitionists and Black residents, the latter of which there were about two hundred in the city, feared that Butman was in town to kidnap another former slave. The city, on high alert and watching his every move, formed a vigilance committee to watch the Temperance Hotel where Butman was staying, according to the Worcester Historical Museum. Butman made the mistake of carrying a concealed weapon, which was against the law in Worcester. He was promptly apprehended by authorities and arrested.

After his hearing, hundreds of citizens gathered to jeer and taunt the reviled Butman. On the steps of City Hall, several Black men charged at him, one striking him on the head and knocking him down, as the *Massachusetts Spy* reported, per the Worcester Historical Museum. There were calls to tar and feather Butman; others called for his death. The *Spy* recounted: "By morning, the crowd was huge and furious. Fearing for his life, Butman asked for protection. It was granted, after he promised never again to come to Worcester. As anti-slavery men escorted him out of town, he suffered punches, kicks and a lot of well-deserved verbal abuse and assault with eggs and other objects. This was the last attempt to execute the Fugitive Slave Law in Massachusetts."

The mob might have killed Butman on the spot had Higginson, Stephen Symonds Foster and George Hoar, an abolitionist and future U.S.

congressman and senator, not pleaded for calm. The three men escorted Butman out of town on the promise that he never return to Worcester. It was a small victory for Higginson and Worcester's abolitionists to defend their turf from the slave hunter. But in the larger scheme of things, the anti-slavery forces were still losing the war.

In 1857, the rights of slaves suffered a major blow when the U.S. Supreme Court voted against Illinois slave Dred Scott, who had sued the federal government for his freedom. As Higginson said in his sermon, the mounting frustrations were enough to turn Free Soilers into "disunionists." Disunionists were in favor of splitting the nation in two: Free States and Slave States. This was, of course, the reverse of what happened in the Civil War, when the South wanted to break free from the North to retain its right to have slaves.

Higginson was one of the leaders of this disunion movement, organizing a "Disunion Convention" in Worcester on January 15, 1857. The convention followed the election of Democrat James Buchanan as president, which many abolitionists saw as the final straw. Buchanan believed in popular sovereignty, or allowing states to decide for themselves on slavery. The convention, attended by about one hundred people, took place at City Hall for the purpose of considering the separation of the Free and Slave States. According to the *Proceedings of the State Disunion Convention*:

We, the undersigned, citizens of Worcester, believing the result of the recent Presidential Election to involve four years more of Pro-Slavery Government, and a rapid increase in the hostility between the two sections of the Union: Believing this hostility to be the offspring, not of party excitement, but of a fundamental difference in education, habits, and laws: Believing the existing Union to be a failure, as being a hopeless attempt to unite under one government two antagonistic systems of society, which diverge more widely with every year: And believing it to be the duty of intelligent and conscientious men to meet these facts with wisdom and firmness: Respectfully invite our fellow citizens of Massachusetts to meet in Convention at Worcester, on Thursday, Jan. 15, to consider the practicability, probability, and expediency, of a Separation between the Free and Slave States, and to take such other measures as the condition of the times may require.

Higginson, who was president of the convention, struck a defeated but defiant tone in his address. It contained the seeds of the epic struggle to come in the next few years during the Civil War.

Well, friends, the battle has been fought, politically, against the extension of slavery. It has been fought and lost. No intelligent man doubts that. The verdict of the country has been given unequivocally in favor of the extension of slavery. It cannot be denied that this is the practical result of the last campaign. The only question now is, what are we to do? Are we to stand still those of us who act under the Constitution—and fight over dead issues, as the Whig party did over banks, tariffs, and sub-treasuries, or are we, as intelligent, progressive men, to prepare to meet the coming crisis? I hold that our duty, as Republicans, is to prepare for the future. It seems to me that the antagonism is necessary, inevitable, and that unless slavery is speedily abolished, a separation, in some form or other, must come.

The attendees approved several resolutions, including one calling for a national disunion convention among the Free States. Higginson, William Lloyd Garrison, Daniel Mann and Wendell Phillips sent out letters in July 1857 seeking to organize a national convention in the fall of 1857, according to Margaret Hope Bacon's book on Kelley, but it was cancelled due to the financial panic that was going on at the time.

While the national version of the disunion convention never happened, the local disunion gathering in Worcester showed how tensions had risen to the point of no return—not just among southerners, but northerners as well. Worcester, once again, was at the forefront of massive social change.

Higginson would never recede from the fight, despite his frustrations. In fact, he became more determined than ever to end slavery, joining the cause of radical abolitionist John Brown. Higginson was one of Brown's Secret Six—wealthy backers from Massachusetts and New York who funded Brown's raids to free slaves. Following the Kansas-Nebraska Act of 1854, which said that the people of those states should vote to decide whether or not to be Slave States, Brown led a group of volunteers, including two men from Worcester—Charles Plummer Tidd and Dr. Calvin Cutter—to Kansas to attack slave owners and free their slaves. These attacks became known as "Bleeding Kansas."

After the Bleeding Kansas raids, Brown, who was born in Torrington, Connecticut, and lived for a spell in Springfield, Massachusetts, had been planning his next crusade to free slaves. Brown visited Worcester in March 1857 to attend a speech by Frederick Douglass. Brown met with Higginson in Worcester as well, looking to raise money for his next "most important" attack. He followed that up with a letter to Higginson on February 2, 1858, from Rochester, as Higginson detailed in his book *Cheerful Yesterdays*.

My Dear Sir, I am here concealing my whereabouts for good reasons (as I think) not however from any anxiety about my personal safety. I have been told that you are both a true man: and a true abolitionist; and I partly believe the whole story. Last fall I undertook to raise from $500 to $1000, for secret service and succeeded in getting $500.

I now want to get for the perfecting of BY FAR the most important undertaking of my whole life; from $500 to $800 within the next sixty days….Can you be induced to operate at Worcester and elsewhere during that time to raise from anti-slavery men and women (or any other parties) some part of that amount? I wish to keep it entirely still about where I am; and will be greatly obliged if you will consider this communication strictly confidential: unless it may be with such as you are sure will feel and act and keep very still….Should be most happy to meet you again; and talk matters more freely. Hope this is my last effort in the begging line. Very Respectfully your friend—John Brown.

The "most important undertaking" Brown referenced in the letter was the ill-fated raid on Harpers Ferry, Virginia, in 1859, when he attempted to take over an arsenal and lead a slave revolt. The revolt failed, and Brown was charged with treason, murder and insurrection and sentenced to death by hanging. Higginson met with the Brown family in North Elba, New York, to bring Brown's wife down to Virginia to see him in prison before he was hanged. Higginson also provided Brown's family with financial and emotional support. He even considered a plan to kidnap the Virginia governor and release him only when Brown was set free. But the rescue plan never happened, and Brown was hanged on December 2, 1859, in Charlestown, Virginia (now West Virginia). Just before he died, Brown wrote to Higginson from his prison cell, "Truly you have proved yourself to be a friend in need."

While the other five members of the Secret Six fled to Europe or Canada to avoid possible prosecution once word got out that Brown had financial backers, Higginson refused to run. He stood his ground and continued to publicly support Brown and his cause. Higginson was never tried or even asked to testify for backing Brown, to his own great surprise. "I think it was a disappointment to me not to be summoned to testify before the [Senate] Committee, nor do I know why I was passed over, after Wilson's assurance. Certainly, I should have told them all I knew and whether that would have done good or harm, I cannot now say," Higginson wrote to a friend in 1860, per Higginson's biography, *Thomas Wentworth Higginson:*

Author and abolitionist Edward Everett Hale was the minister of the Unitarian Church in Worcester. His most famous work is "The Man without a Country," written to inspire patriotism during the Civil War. *National Portrait Gallery, Smithsonian Institution.*

The Story of His Life, written by his wife, Mary Potter Higginson. "So far as John Brown is concerned, I should like this for an epitaph, 'The only one of John Brown's friends and advisers who was not frightened by the silly threats of Hugh Forbes into desiring that year's delay which ruined the enterprise.' I had the old man's own assurance that in his secret soul he regarded this delay as an act of timidity and acted on it only because those who held the purse insisted."

Higginson was referring to one of the influential soldiers in John Brown's volunteer army, Hugh Forbes, who had called to delay the raid on Harpers Ferry from 1858 to 1859 to raise more money, which Higginson opposed but Brown acquiesced to. Higginson saw this as the reason for the failed insurrection, per Mary Potter Higginson's book.

Ultimately, Higginson and the abolitionists would be on the right side of history. In just a few short years, President Lincoln signed the Emancipation Proclamation and freed all slaves. Higginson fought for the North in the Civil War to preserve the union, leading a battalion of Black soldiers, which he detailed in his book *Army Life in a Black Regiment*.

Higginson was a prolific writer, authoring numerous books and articles. He was a contemporary and friend of Edward Everett Hale, the famous author and abolitionist who was the minister of the Unitarian Church of the Unity in Worcester from 1846 to 1856 before he moved back to Boston. His most famous work is the short story "The Man without a Country," written to inspire patriotism during the Civil War. While in Worcester, Hale co-founded the New England Emigrant Aid Company to help immigrants from Free States settle in Kansas. He was also a historian and a lifetime member of the American Antiquarian Society.

In his later years, Higginson was a mentor of sorts to another great writer, Emily Dickinson. He published an article in the *Atlantic Monthly* magazine calling on young writers to step up and make their voices heard. One of those young writers was Dickinson, a thirty-two-year-old writer from Amherst, Massachusetts. Dickinson, who would become one of America's greatest poets, sought feedback from Higginson on her poems. Higginson, who would serve as a lifelong friend and mentor to Dickinson, was blown away by her talent, as he wrote in the *Atlantic Monthly* in 1891. "The impression of a wholly new and original poetic genius was as distinct on my mind at the first reading of these four poems as it is now, after thirty years of further knowledge; and with it came the problem never yet solved, what place ought to be assigned in literature to what is so remarkable, yet so elusive of criticism."

8

WORCESTER

A Pioneer for Women's Rights

Many of the Worcester revolutionaries who championed the abolition of slavery were also at the vanguard of the burgeoning women's rights movement. Abby Kelley Foster, who broke barriers as a speaker against slavery, was one of the founding mothers of the women's movement, not just in Worcester, but in the entire country. So was Lucy Stone, who was from nearby West Brookfield.

Like Kelley, Stone was a champion of women's rights and the abolition of slavery and toured the country as an orator, making her first speech in Gardner, Massachusetts, where her brother was a pastor at the former Evangelical Congregational Church on Green Street, as the *Gardner News* reported. A stone marker honoring her sits at 186 Elm Street in Gardner, where her sister Sarah lived and Lucy sometimes stayed.

This pioneer was the first woman in Massachusetts, and one of the first women in the country, to earn a college degree, graduating from Oberlin College in 1847. Stone was also one of the first women to keep her maiden name after getting married. In addition, Stone was one of the major organizers of the first National Women's Rights Convention, held in Worcester in 1850.

The very first convention for women's rights was established in 1848 in Seneca Falls, New York, by Elizabeth Cady Stanton and Lucretia Mott. Seneca Falls is considered the birthplace of the women's rights movement to this day, but Worcester should also be recognized for its contributions. The Seneca Falls Convention came about after both Stanton and Mott attended

Lucy Stone was one of the leading voices for women's rights and one of the founding mothers of the first National Women's Rights Convention, held in Worcester in 1850. *National Portrait Gallery, Smithsonian Institution.*

a world anti-slavery meeting in London in 1840 with their husbands but were not allowed to participate because they were women. They vowed to change that, which led to the Seneca Falls Convention.

Kelley was not there at Seneca Falls, but she had a connection to the city. Five years earlier, in 1843, Kelley was on a speaking tour in Upstate New York, and one of her stops was Seneca Falls. She gave six speeches that August week in 1843, three of them outside because the churches would not let her inside. As was typical for Kelley, she did not hold back her disgust toward the churches, as the New England Historical Society reported. "This nation is guilty of slavery. It is a sin. Your churches are connected with slavery, and they are guilty of that sin. They are not Christians if they are slaveholders, if they steal and sell men, women and children, if they rob cradles."

Kelley asked the attendees to sign a pledge to refuse to support any church, minister or politician who supported slavery or who associated with people who held slaves. She was heckled and had rotten eggs thrown at her, but she also found many supporters in this growing hotbed for social reform. The community in the Finger Lakes region of New York attracted Boston journalist and social reformer Henry Stanton, who moved there with his wife, Elizabeth Cady Stanton, in 1847. A year later, Elizabeth would organize the Seneca Falls Convention and introduce her Declaration of Sentiments for Women's Rights, a seminal document in the movement.

The goal of that first convention in Seneca Falls was to follow it with a series of events to bring it to a national audience. Over the next year or two, women's rights conventions were held in Rochester, New York, and in Ohio, but it wasn't until 1850 that the first in a series of national conventions came about in Worcester, thanks in large part to Stone. Stone was a driving force behind its establishment, inspired by the Ohio Women's Convention, which she attended in April 1850 in Salem, Ohio. At that meeting, the delegation sent a letter to the Ohio state government urging leaders to hold a constitutional convention to give women the same political and legal rights as men. Stone thought this was a great idea and was determined to do the same in her home state of Massachusetts. "Massachusetts ought to have taken the lead in the work you are now doing, but if she chooses to linger, let her young sisters of the West set her a worthy example; and if the 'Pilgrim spirit is not dead,' we'll pledge Massachusetts to follow her," Stone wrote to the Ohio conference organizers, according to the proceedings from the convention.

The "Pilgrim spirit" was indeed alive and well in Massachusetts, as plans for a national convention took shape at the annual meeting of the American Anti-Slavery Society, which took place in Boston from May 28 to May 30, 1850, at Melodeon Hall and Faneuil Hall. It was during this meeting that Stone, Kelley Foster, Paulina Wright Davis and a few others called for an annual national women's convention, according to Andrea Moore Kerr in her book *Lucy Stone: Speaking Out for Equality*. Stone and Davis took the lead, organizing a meeting to be held immediately after the Anti-Slavery Society meeting ended on May 30 at Melodeon Hall to plan the event. William Lloyd Garrison, the publisher of the *Liberator* and leader of the American Anti-Slavery Society, was among the eleven people in attendance at that planning meeting. "I conceive that the first thing to be done by the women of this country is to demand their political enfranchisement. Among the 'self-evident truths' announced in the Declaration of Independence is this—'All government derives its just power from the consent of the governed,'" Garrison said, according to his biography.

Stone, Kelley Foster, Davis and Garrison were joined at the meeting by Dr. Harriot Hunt, Eliza and Dora Taft, Eliza Kendall and Wendell Phillips. Stone was the secretary, and Kelley Foster was part of the committee on arrangements. It chose Worcester as the site of the inaugural convention. Worcester was a center of trade with a rich cultural scene, and it was easily accessible by train, according to Jessie Rodrique with the Worcester Women's History Project. Also, Worcester had long been established as a "seething center" of social reforms, as Higginson once put it.

As John McClymer detailed in his book *This High and Holy Moment: The First National Women's Right's Convention, Worcester, 1850*, all of Worcester's candidates for office in the 1850s were anti-slavery. It was also a hotbed for the burgeoning temperance movement, championed by John Bartholomew Gough of Boylston, one of the nation's leading advocates for temperance and a persuasive orator on the topic. Gough House, where this important figure lived at 215 Main Street in Boylston, is listed in the National Register of Historic Places.

It was also the home of two of the nation's most prominent women's rights leaders in Kelley and Stone, along with other prominent activists, like Abby Price of nearby Hopedale. The city had indeed built quite a reputation. "The Whigs, Democrats, Free-Democrats, Land Reformers, Come-Outers and Disunionists have already held their respective Conventions for the season, and most of them in this city," an 1850 article in Worcester's *National Aegis* newspaper stated, according to McClymer.

Davis put out a call to announce the convention, as McClymer detailed in his book. The opening paragraph of the call stated: "A convention will be held at Worcester, Mass., on the twenty-third and twenty-fourth of October next, (agreeably to appointment by a preliminary meeting held at Boston, on the thirtieth of May last) to consider the great question of Women's Rights, Duties, and Relations: and the Men and Women in our country who feel sufficient interest in the subject, to give an earnest thought and effective effort to its rightful adjustment, are invited to meet each other in free conference, at the time and place appointed." The announcement continued: "It is your duty, if you are worthy of your age and country. Give the help of your best thought to separate the light from the darkness. Wisely give the protection of your name and the benefit of your efforts to the great work of settling the principles, devising the method, and achieving the success of this high and holy movement."

Davis and Stone were on the committee of correspondence, charged with recruiting speakers and attendees. "We need all the women who are accustomed to speak in public—every stick of timber that is sound," Stone wrote to Antoinette Brown, a fellow Oberlin student. Similar letters were written to other women leaders, including Lucretia Mott, according to the book *Friends and Sisters: Letters between Lucy Stone and Antoinette Brown Blackwell, 1846–93*.

In the months leading up to the convention, Stone caught typhoid fever while traveling to Indiana to visit her brother, who was ill and who ultimately died. On the way back to Massachusetts, Stone got the fever and nearly died herself. She was forced to step back from organizing the convention in the final weeks, leaving it mostly to Davis. However, she was strong enough to attend the convention. She had limited participation, but she did address the crowd as a speaker. Meanwhile, Garrison and Phillips also helped generate interest among their contacts. Ultimately, the outreach efforts secured eighty-nine enthusiastic supporters, many of them convention organizers and speakers, along with others, like Ralph Waldo Emerson, who were champions of the cause.

The convention was held October 23–24, 1850, at Brinley Hall in Worcester with about one thousand people in attendance—including men and women. Delegates came from eleven different states. Along with Stone, speakers included William Lloyd Garrison, William Henry Channing, Wendell Phillips, Harriot Kezia Hunt, Ernestine Rose, Antoinette Brown, Sojourner Truth, Stephen Symonds Foster, Abby Kelley Foster, Abby Price, Lucretia Mott and Frederick Douglass.

The newspaper accounts said the streets surrounding Brinley Hall were overflowing with delegates. According to the website Mass Moments, the *New York Tribune* reported: "There must have been over a thousand people present through nearly all the meetings. If a larger place could have been had many thousand more would have attended. Many have gone away, not being able to fund admission." The article continued: "The room was crowded to excess, every seat, and aisle, and the space around the platform, being filled, men and women standing on their feet during the whole evening. A heartfelt interest evidently pervaded the audience."

Davis presided over the convention and was the event's first speaker. "We cannot be too careful or too brave, too gentle or too firm; and yet with right dispositions and honest efforts, we cannot fail of doing our share of the great work, and thereby advancing the highest interest of humanity," Davis said in her opening remarks.

One of the speakers was Abby Price from Hopedale, Massachusetts. While her works were never published in any books, Price was considered a brilliant poet and was the

Paulina Wright Davis was one of the main organizers of the Worcester women's rights convention, which she presided over. She was also the first speaker. *Library of Congress Prints and Photographs Division.*

poet laureate of her community, according to Price biographer Susan G. LaMar. Price was an ardent feminist and was friends with Kelley, Stone, Paulina Davis and many other women's rights activists of her day. Price spoke at the first two National Women's Conventions in Worcester, as well as at the third, which took place in Syracuse, and the fourth, in New York City. Price later moved to New York City, where, in 1856, she became close friends with poet Walt Whitman, the year after he published *Leaves of Grass*. Price corresponded frequently with Whitman, and he often visited her and stayed with her family. She is described by one of Whitman's biographers as "one of Whitman's dearest confidantes." She had a great influence on Whitman's work, as author Sherry Ceniza described in her book *Walt Whitman and the 19th Century Women Reformers*.

> *There can be no convincing critical work on Whitman and women if the ties he had with the woman's rights movement are not taken into account. Because of the woman's movement and the women in his life, Whitman became more sensitized to the issue of women and American democracy.... Also, of importance is the extensive oratory carried on by activists for woman's rights in the decade of the 1850s. When one notes the importance that oratory played in Whitman's mind and writing, the presence of such orators-activists-friends as Price, Davis, Rose cannot be ignored.*

At the first National Women's Rights Convention in Worcester, Price delivered a powerful speech—one of the few from that inaugural convention published by the Library of Congress and recorded in the *Proceedings of the Woman's Rights Convention*.

> *In contending for this co-equality of woman's with man's rights, it is not necessary to argue, either that the sexes are by nature equally and indiscriminately adapted to the same positions and duties, or that they are absolutely equal in physical and intellectual ability; but only that they are absolutely equal in their rights to life, liberty, and the pursuit of happiness—in their rights to do, and to be, individually and socially, all they are capable of, and to attain the highest usefulness and happiness, obediently to the divine moral law.... To repress them in any degree is in the same degree usurpation, tyranny, and oppression.*

In her address, Stone urged attendees to petition their state legislatures for the right of suffrage and the right of married women to hold property. "We want to be something more than the appendages of Society; we want that Woman should be the coequal and help-meet of Man in all the interest and perils and enjoyments of human life. We want that she should attain to the development of her nature and womanhood; we want that when she dies, it may not be written on her gravestone that she was the 'relict' of somebody," Stone said, according to the New England Historical Society.

Stone's speech left a deep impression on a woman named Susan B. Anthony, a teacher from Rochester, New York. Anthony did not attend the convention, but she read about it in newspaper accounts and in pamphlets that Stone herself printed and distributed at her lectures after the convention. Anthony was said to be inspired by Stone's words to get more actively involved in the cause, according to *Time* magazine. In 1852 in Syracuse, Anthony did attend the third National Women's Rights Convention and was once again inspired by Stone's speech, this time in person, according to the National Park Service. Anthony would, of course, become the champion of the women's rights movement when she was arrested in 1872 for voting in Rochester. As Elizabeth Cady Stanton said in her later years, "Lucy Stone was the first person by whom the heart of the American public was deeply stirred on the woman question," according to Stone's biographer Alice Stone Blackwell.

That first national convention in Worcester included several resolutions that defined the movement's objective, per the *Proceedings*.

> *Resolved, That women are clearly entitled to the right of suffrage, and to be considered eligible to office; the omission to demand which, on her part, is a palpable recreancy to duty; and the denial of which is a gross usurpation, on the part of man, no longer to be endured; and that every party which claims to represent the humanity, civilization, and progress of the age, is bound to inscribe on its banners, Equality before the law, without distinction of sex or color.*

They also approved resolutions that said the word *male* should be stricken from every state constitution and that wives have "an equal control over the property gained by their mutual toil and sacrifices."

Stanton also did not attend that inaugural convention, as she was in the late stages of pregnancy. However, she was appointed to the Education Committee and sent along a letter of support, per the *Proceedings*.

> *Some tell us that if woman should interest herself in political affairs, it would destroy all domestic harmony. What, say they, would be the*

consequence, if husband and wife should not agree in their views of political economy?...Because she might choose to deposit her vote for righteous rulers—such as love, justice, mercy, truth, and oppose a husband, father, or brother, who would, by their votes, place political power in the hands of unprincipled men, swearing, fighting, leaders of armies, rumsellers and drunkards, slaveholders and 52 prating northern hypocrites, who would surrender the poor panting fugitive from bondage into the hands of his blood-thirsty pursuers—shall she not vote at all? It is high time that men learned to tolerate independence of thought and opinion in the women of their household.

Abby Kelley Foster delivered a fiery speech that even many of the convention organizers found "odious," as Stone recalled, according to McClymer. The *New York Herald* detailed her speech in its October 25, 1850 edition, documented by McClymer and Assumption College's Women's History Workshop.

I do not talk of woman's rights, but of human rights, the rights of human beings. I do not come to ask [for] them, but to demand them; not to get down on my knees and beg for them, but to claim them. Sauce for the goose is sauce for the gander. We have our rights, and the right to revolt, as did our fathers against King George the Third—the right to rise up and cut the tyrants' throats. On this subject I scorn to talk like a woman. We must give them the truth, and not twaddle. We must not be mealy mouthed with our tyrants in broadcloth and tight clothes.

Kelley also said, according to the article, "that all distinction in society between man and woman should be abolished, and that a woman was just as well qualified to be President as a man."

The newspaper accounts of this first convention were mostly negative, demeaning and hostile. The *New York Herald* called it an "awful combination of socialism, abolitionism, and infidelity. The Pantalettes striking for the Pantaloons. Bible and Constitution repudiated." In an account from the second day, October 25, the *Herald* mocked one of the speakers, Ernestine Rose, a suffragist who emigrated from Poland and had an accent. The reporter wrote of Rose's speech: "Mrs. Rose spoke at some length, saying, among other things, dat woman is in de quality of de slave, and day man is de tyrant; and dat when de distinction of rights between de sexes ceases, then, and not till then, will woman get her just desserts."

The *Herald*, whose editor was James Gordon Bennett, published a vicious wrap-up of the convention on October 28, referring to it as the "Piebald fanatics of the North," as McClymer detailed in his book. (The newspaper accounts that follow come courtesy of McClymer through his book and his Women's History Workshop website at Assumption College.) The *Herald* editorial read as follows:

> *That motley gathering of fanatical mongrels, of old grannies, male and female, of fugitive slaves and fugitive lunatics, called the Woman's Rights Convention, after two day's discussion of the most horrible trash, has put forth its platform and adjourned. The sentiments and doctrines avowed, and the social revolution projected, involve all the most monstrous and disgusting principles of socialism, abolition, amalgamation, and infidelity. The full consummation of their diabolical projects would reduce society to the most beastly and promiscuous confusion—the most disgusting barbarism that could be devised; and the most revolting familiarities of equality and licentiousness between whites and blacks, of both sexes, that lunatics and demons could invent.... There is not a lunatic asylum in the country, wherein, if the inmates were called together in sit in convention, they would not exhibit more sense, reason, decency and delicacy, and less of lunacy, blasphemy, and horrible sentiments, than this hybrid, mongrel, pie-bald, crack-brained, pitiful, disgusting and ridiculous assemblage. And there we drop them, and may God have mercy on their miserable souls. Amen.*

History has indeed not been kind to Bennett and the *Herald* for their noxious views.

The *Boston Daily Mail* was equally as denigrating, calling it "a grand demonstration of petticoatdom at Worcester" in its headline. The *Daily Mail*'s account of day two's speeches was snide and dismissive. "There was a very industrious hum and bustle during all the time [Stephen] Foster spoke. Abby [Kelley, Foster's wife] chimed in, and told an anecdote about something we could not catch the skirt of. It was something concerning the impolicy of women obeying their husbands. Hasn't Foster caught a Tartar? Heaven preserve all mankind from these dreadfully wise women, who know all about politics and nothing about sewing and darning! The two emptied the Hall well, between them."

But history indeed reflects favorably on other news outlets that recognized the historical importance of this gathering. One of them was the local paper, the *Spy*, whose editor at the time, John Milton Earle, was the husband of Sarah Hussey Earle, one of the organizers of the convention. She delivered the opening remarks. On the opening address by Davis, the *Spy* wrote, "The address was elaborate, evincing much and deep reflection, and was written with great clearness and even elegance of style. As a mere literary composition, it was very credible to the author."

Another positive account was published by the *Liberator*, run by organizer and speaker Garrison.

God bless all these noble men and women and raise up more like them to labor in the great work of universal reformation, unity and happiness! Meanwhile, may all those who were present at the Convention and sympathizing with it, cherish the holy and sublime aspirations and purposes awakened within them, and unitedly and continually labor for the realization of what they long for! By and by, those who mean to be the doers of the word, as well as hearers and speakers of it, will organise Communities on the principles of justice and equality, in harmony with the law of celestial love. Let us hope on and ever. There is "a good time coming." The kingdom of God draweth near!

The influential *New York Daily Tribune*, published by abolitionist and former congressman Horace Greeley, gave the fullest account of the convention, with reports daily on all of the speakers, including Sojourner Truth, the former slave and abolitionist who made her first-ever address on women's rights at Worcester, according to McClymer. It was one of the high moments of the convention and "gratified the audience highly."

The *Tribune* also provided details of the address delivered by Frederick Douglass, one of the great orators of his day.

Sojourner Truth, the former slave who became a leading voice against slavery, made her first speech for women's rights at the Worcester convention. *Schomburg Center for Research in Black Culture, Photographs and Prints Division, The New York Public Library.* "*I sell the shadow to support the substance, Sojourner Truth.*" *New York Public Library Digital Collections.*

He said, "this Convention has now been in session two days, and no one has attempted to offer anything against the sentiments and principles advanced here. It is not because there is no opposition to this movement; but because the truths on which it is founded are invulnerable. The arguments advanced cannot be met except by ridicule, and this will be the great weapon that will be used against us."...He closed by urging strongly that women should take their rights. "Seize hold of those which are most strongly contested. You have already free access to the paths of literature; Women may write books of poetry, travels, et cetera and they will be read avidly. Let them strike out in some other path where they are not now allowed to go. If there is some kind of business from which they are excluded, let some heroic woman enter upon that business, as some of these noble Women have entered upon the practice of medicine. Let Woman take her rights, and then she shall be free."

Greeley, who would later run for president and lose in 1870, responded to a letter to the editor about the convention in the November 2, 1850 edition.

We heartily rejoice that the Women's Rights Convention was held and trust it will be followed by others. Our correspondent admits that Woman endures great wrongs which cry aloud for redress but thinks the Worcester Convention misunderstood both the disease and the remedy. Very well, let the discussion go on, until wiser heads shall be interested and safer counsels prevail. For our part, we are well satisfied with the general scope and bearing of the Worcester discussions, and trust they will be followed up.

This first convention indeed helped to create a dialogue on women's rights and inspired women locally, nationally and around the world. Jeanne Deroin and Pauline Roland, two French women who were imprisoned in Paris for their political activities, sent a letter that was read into the record at the second Women's National Convention, which also took place in Worcester the next year, 1851. According to the *Proceedings*, published by the Library of Congress: "Dear Sisters: Your courageous declaration of Woman's Rights has resounded even to our prison and has filled our souls with inexpressible joy. In France, the Re-action has suppressed the cry of Liberty of the Women of the future, deprived, like their brothers of the Democracy, of the right to civil and political equality; and the fiscal laws, which trammel the liberty of the press, hinder the propagation of those eternal truths which must regenerate humanity."

The second National Women's Rights Convention returned to Worcester in 1851, held at the same place, Brinley Hall, on October 15 and 16. It was an even bigger event than the first. It was run by many of the same individuals, with Davis once again serving as president and lead organizer.

REPORT

OF THE

SECOND GENERAL CONVENTION

OF

FRIENDS OF WOMAN'S RIGHTS.

Wednesday, October 15th, 1851.

MORNING SESSION.

IN accordance with a call from the Central Committee, appointed by the Convention of 1850, the Friends of Woman's Rights assembled in Worcester, at Brinley Hall, on Wednesday morning, Oct. 15, 1851. At an early hour the hall was filled.

The meeting was called to order by the chief of the Central Committee, Paulina W. Davis; who, upon motion of Dr. J. F. Flagg, of Boston, was appointed President *pro tem.*

The following list of Officers for the Convention was then presented, and unanimously adopted :—

President.

PAULINA W. DAVIS, ... Providence, R. I.

Vice Presidents.

ANGELINA GRIMKE WELD, ... New Jersey.
WM. H. CHANNING, ... Boston.
SAMUEL J. MAY, ... Syracuse.
C. I. H. NICHOLS, ... Vermont.
LUCRETIA MOTT, ... Philadelphia.

Secretaries.

ANNA Q. T. PARSONS, ... Boston.
GEO. W. PUTNAM, ... Lynn.

A copy of the proceedings from the second Women's Rights Convention in Worcester, 1851. *Retrieved from the Library of Congress.*

The various committees established the previous year provided updates on their progress and activities. Among the speakers at this second convention was Abby Kelley Foster, the event's final presenter. She delivered another powerful speech, offering a call to action, as detailed in the *Proceedings*.

For fourteen years I have advocated this cause by my daily life. Bloody feet, sisters, have worn smooth the path by which you have come up hither. (Great sensation.) You will not need to speak when you speak by your everyday life. Oh, how truly does Webster say, Action, action, is eloquence! Let us, then, when we go home, go not to complain, but to work. Do not go home to complain of the men but go and make greater exertions than ever to discharge your every-day duties. Oh! it is easy to be lazy; it is comfortable indeed to be indolent; but it is hard, and a martyrdom, to take responsibilities. There are thousands of women in these United States working for a starving pittance, who know and feel that they are fitted for something better, and who tell me, when I talk to them, and urge them to open shops, and do business for themselves, "I do not want the responsibility of business—it is too much." Well, then, starve in your laziness! Oh, Madam President, I feel that we have thrown too much blame on the other side. At any rate, we all deserve enough. We have been groping about in the dark. We are trying to feel our way, and oh! God give us light! But I am convinced that as we go forward and enter the path, it will grow brighter and brighter unto the perfect day.

After those first two years in Worcester, the convention moved to other sites across the country as the movement continued to grow. While the Seneca Falls Convention is seen as the birth of the movement, the Worcester conventions are of great historical significance, according to none other than Elizabeth Cady Stanton. She spoke at the opening session of the 1870 Woman's Rights Convention in New York City, according to the Worcester Women's History Project: "The movement in England, as in America, may be dated from the first National Convention, held at Worcester, Mass., October 1850."

Three years after that first convention, there was a petition at the Massachusetts Constitutional Convention in 1853 that the word *male* be stricken from the constitution. This was one of the goals of the first convention, so the impact of these gatherings was evident. Worcester County voted almost two to one in favor of the constitutional amendments, but the petition was defeated, according to the Worcester Women's History Project. But it is another example of how progressive the Worcester region

ABBY KELLEY FOSTER.
Published at the Arch St. Gallery of the Daguerreotype Philadelphia

Abby Kelley Foster delivered speeches at both women's rights conventions in Worcester in 1850 and 1851. *Library of Congress Prints and Photographs Division.*

was on this issue, as well as on slavery. But two years later, in 1855, progress was made. Laws were passed allowing women to keep their property after marriage and keep their own wages, according to the Worcester Women's History Project.

Kelley remained a vocal supporter for women's rights, helping to organize the New England Woman Suffrage Association in 1868. She died on January 14, 1887, and is buried at Hope Cemetery in Worcester. She was inducted into the National Women's Hall of Fame in 2011. Stone went on to be one of the founders of the American Woman Suffrage Association in 1869 and published the *Woman's Journal* in 1870. She was inducted into the National Women's Hall of Fame in 1986.

That "perfect day" that Kelley talked about at the second convention would not come until 1920, when women earned the right to vote. Her call for a female president has still not come to fruition, but the battle goes on.

9

CLARA BARTON AND THE HEROES

OF THE CIVIL WAR

There were many heroes from Worcester who fought to preserve the union during the Civil War, but few were more valiant than George Hull Ward, who died in the seminal Battle of Gettysburg, where a memorial honoring him stands on the battlefield to this day.

Ward was born on April 26, 1826, in Worcester, where he grew up on his family's farm on Green Street. In 1847, at the age of twenty-one, Ward joined the Worcester City Guard, a volunteer militia that assisted local law enforcement. City Guards were fairly common in antebellum days, but they were eventually eliminated in favor of the National Guard structure. While serving in the City Guard, Ward worked in a textile mill and raised a family with his wife, Emily Mayo.

George Ward had risen to the rank of brigadier general in the City Guard, but shortly after rebel soldiers attacked Fort Sumter on April 12, 1861, launching the Civil War, the thirty-five-year-old joined the Union army. With his experience and leadership with the City Guard, Ward was made lieutenant colonel of the Massachusetts Fifteenth Regiment, second in command under General Charles Devens of Worcester. According to Abijah Marvin's book *The History of Worcester in the War of the Rebellion*, Devens said at a ceremonial sendoff for the Fifteenth Regiment on August 7 at City Hall, hosted by Senator George Hoar:

> *There is indeed, a remarkable coincidence, as you have so well said, in the name of the regiment which I have the honor to command, being numbered the same as that commanded during the revolutionary war, by Colonel*

Timothy Bigelow, over whose remains yonder proud monument was, three months ago, erected with such inspiring ceremonies. It is indeed a most fortunate omen. I trust that some of the spirit which animated our ancestors, has descended upon the present sons of Worcester County, and that they will be able to render an equally good account of their labors.

The next day, the 1,046 soldiers from the Fifteenth Regiment headed for the banks of the Potomac River in Loudon County, Virginia, to join the Union army, commanded there by General Charles Stone. A few months after they arrived, in late October, they were engaged in one of the most disastrous battles of the war to that point. On October 20, 1861, Stone sent a troop of men across the Potomac to scout out the area. The leader of the expedition, Captain Chase Philbrick, reported back to Stone that he saw an unguarded Confederate camp, but what he thought were tents was actually a stand of trees.

A few hours later, Stone sent one of his best regiments, the Massachusetts Fifteenth, led by Devens and Ward, to attack the unsuspecting Confederate camp. Under Ward's leadership, the regiment was considered one of the most disciplined and effective in the army. But when Devens arrived with his three hundred men, he found no camp there, as it had been mistakenly identified by Philbrick. So Devens stayed there, awaiting further instructions from Stone via messenger if he should push forward toward Leesburg. But while he waited, a Confederate company in the area got word that the Union army was nearby and launched its own attack. The Confederate troops had the element of surprise, and the Massachusetts Fifteenth was caught flat-footed.

The Confederate company routed the Union troops at Ball's Bluff, literally driving many of them over the bluffs into the Potomac to their deaths. One of the casualties was Colonel Edward Baker, a U.S. senator from Oregon. He remains the only sitting congressman to die in battle. The Massachusetts Fifteenth suffered greatly, as forty-four of its ranks died at Ball's Bluff and many more were injured, including Ward. Shot in the leg and incapacitated, he was carried off the battlefield to safety, but to save his life, his leg had to be amputated below the knee. Ward bore the operation bravely, but it "was a sad sight," said an eyewitness, "to see a brave officer in that position," according to Abijah Marvin's book.

Marvin wrote: "The losses of the regiment in killed, wounded, drowned and prisoners, was very great, hardly surpassed in any case during the war. Of the six hundred and twenty-one men who went into the battle, but three

A depiction of the Battle at Ball's Bluff, where Worcester Civil War hero George Hull Ward lost his leg. *Library of Congress Prints and Photographs Division.*

hundred and eleven were left fit for duty. The killed, wounded and missing were three hundred and ten."

George Ward wrote constantly to his wife, Emily, and two kids while away at war, particularly while he was recuperating from his amputation. Many of their correspondences are preserved in the archives at the Worcester Historical Museum. One of those preserved letters, published in *Worcester Magazine*, was about Ward's injury at Ball's Bluff, as he informed his wife of the bad news.

My dear wife, I have suffered in the cause I came forth to uphold yet I know not how to be thankful enough that my life is spared. I was wounded in my left leg and it was so badly splintered that they amputated it about half way between the knee and ankle. A loss, dear one, but how much worse it might have been in the dreadful carnage we have been called to bear....Do not be over anxious dear one and a few weeks shall unite us again. With many kisses to my dear ones and love unbonded, I remain yours forever.

Ward recuperated for several months in Maryland. While in recovery, he received a letter from his wife. "I can't be thankful enough that you are safe. You can possibly do without your left foot, but I couldn't do without you, my dear husband," she wrote. Ward was eventually sent back home, as he was no longer able to fight, but he stayed involved in the effort, recruiting men for the Fifteenth Regiment. However, Ward longed to return to the battlefield to fight alongside his men. It pained him deeply that some three hundred of his men were lost in the bloody battle at Antietam on September 17, 1862.

Ward reenlisted in January 1863 despite the objections of friends and family, who urged him to retire. On his one good leg, he rejoined his men at Falmouth, Virginia, along the Rappahannock River, where the Union army made its winter quarters. Ward was named a brigadier general, commanding troops that fought at the Battle of Fredericksburg on May 2 at Mary's Heights. It was a successful campaign with very few casualties for the Union.

From there, Ward and the Fifteenth Regiment made the long march to Gettysburg, Pennsylvania, to help the Union army hold off the advancing Confederates. It would be the bloodiest battle of the war and one of the deadliest in American history. Ward wrote to his wife in a letter dated June 27 from Poolesville, Maryland, the same place he recovered from his amputated leg. It is believed to be his last letter home. It appears here courtesy of *Worcester Magazine*.

> *I am writing this outdoors in the open field. I have just reached down and plucked a leaf of clover which you will find enclosed....I am afraid we have not seen the worst of this rebellion yet and I almost shudder at the thought what we are to pass through before this struggle is over, but I still trust and believe that all things will turn out well....I hope you are well. I think a great deal of you and pray God to take good care of you....I hope to hear from you soon. I shall write to you every opportunity. Kind regards to all, and lots of love and kisses to you and the children. From your dear husband, George.*

By the time the Union troops reached Gettysburg on July 1, 1863, Ward was struggling and in pain from the journey, but he refused to stand aside and abandon his fellow soldiers. Marvin wrote: "He commanded a brigade and was at the head of his men in the thickest and fiercest of the battle on Thursday. He was in Gibbon's Division of the Second Corps. He handled his men with the utmost coolness and skill and fought with the most determined bravery." Ward fought mostly on horseback and had to prop himself up with his sword when he stood. On the second day of battle, July 2, Ward was given the command of a brigade after several commanders, including General John Reynolds, were killed in the first day of fighting.

"His troops arrived at the scene of action about eight o'clock, on the morning of the second day of the fight. They halted about half a mile in rear of the First Corps, which was in line of battle," George Macker, a member of the Fifteenth Regiment, recalled the day, according to Marvin. "About two o'clock we were called into line, and an order from General Meade was read to us, telling us we must fight, for if we lost, all was lost." The contest was opened by Daniel Sickles about four in the afternoon. Not long after, Colonel Ward received orders to take two regiments of his brigade and advance to the front in an open field. One of these regiments was his own, the Fifteenth. The regiment was flanked by the enemy and "was very near being taken. Our loss was very heavy, as we had to stand fire from all directions. At this time, while the colonel was doing all he could to rally the men, he fell."

Ward took a shot in the thigh and went down. The bullet severed his femoral artery. Macker went to his aid and, along with another soldier, carried him off the battlefield to the division hospital, arriving at about 8:00 p.m. According to Macker's account, Ward was wounded in the back of the right knee. Marvin gave the following account:

> *By direction of the surgeon, he was laid under an apple-tree, on hay obtained from a neighboring barn which was full of wounded men. His blankets, taken from his horse, were spread on the hay, and then he was covered by Macker's blanket. Here he rested and drank some water and expressed himself as feeling better. He also drank a little coffee which had been prepared for him. The night was changing into day before any perceptible alteration was visible. Colonel Ward slept several hours. About three o'clock a change was noticed by Macker, who called the surgeon. At half past four in the morning the spirit of the brave and capable soldier passed away. His remains were brought home and were laid in the grave with suitable honors.*

That other soldier who helped him off the battlefield was likely Ward's half brother Henry Ward. Henry's account of the details of George's death was published in the *Massachusetts Spy*, courtesy of the Worcester Historical Museum.

> *He was wounded in the leg by a minnie ball on Thursday, about 6 o'clock P.M. The artery was severed and he bled to death. He fought well. He had*

The memorial on the battlefield at Gettysburg honoring George Hull Ward. *Courtesy of Veggies. Wikimedia Commons.*

sent his horse to the rear, and I felt then, that, if we should be obliged to retreat, it would be all up with him. He was wounded while fighting at the head of his brigade. The fight continued for five hours, and during the confusion we were unable to find him for two hours. I searched all over the battlefield, amid shells and balls, hunting for him. We got him to a hospital about dark. He was insensible, but the surgeon gave him whiskey, which revived him; and he said to the doctor, "I shall not live two hours." After this, his mind was wandering, and he imagined himself at the head of his brigade, commanding troops, and urging them to fight bravely. He died Friday morning at daylight.

Ward died on July 3, 1863, under that apple tree at Gettysburg at the age of thirty-seven. He was one of fifty-one thousand men who died on the battlefield at Gettysburg, and a monument stands there today in his honor. Its inscription reads: "Here fell, mortally wounded, July 2d 1863, George H. Ward, Colonel Commanding 15th Mass. Vols. His comrades and fellow citizens of Worcester raise this memorial of his valor and patriotism."

The Union won the battle, turning back Confederate general Robert E. Lee's attempt to invade the North. Lee retreated south after the defeat, and it proved to be a turning point in the war, thanks to the heroics and bravery of men like Ward and the Massachusetts Fifteenth. Of the 221 men from the Fifteenth Regiment who went into battle at Gettysburg, 37 died and many more were wounded.

The residents of Worcester turned out in droves to honor Ward at his funeral a few days later at the Salem Street Church in Worcester. According to Abijah Marvin, Reverend Thomas St. John said Ward's eulogy:

Let the blessings of Heaven rest upon him. Bright in the galaxy of names making glorious our country's history, shall forever stand proudly the name of Ward. Well might General Sedgwick say, "When I wanted anything done and could not go myself, I sent the Fifteenth Massachusetts, and everything was well done." The best test of their bravery was the fact that in the several battles in which they won such immortal honors, their ranks were so reduced that at their first roll-call after the battle at Gettysburg, but fifty-six were found to answer to their names.

Ward is buried at Rural Cemetery in Worcester. In addition to the memorial stone at Gettysburg, Ward is on the Civil War Soldier's Monument at City Hall in Worcester. Fort Ward in Washington is named after him.

There were several other regiments from the Worcester area, including the Fifty-First, which was led by Colonel Augustus B.R. Sprague, a future mayor of Worcester, and Captain Thomas Higginson, the noted abolitionist and writer. In January 1863, Higginson was promoted to the rank of colonel as he commanded an all-Black regiment, the First South Carolina Volunteer Infantry Regiment—one of the first Black regiments. Higginson's brigade was made up of escaped and freed slaves from South Carolina and Florida. They mainly fought in battles along the Georgia and Florida coasts. Higginson published a book on his experience, *Army Life in a Black Regiment.* "We, their officers, did not go there to teach lessons, but to receive them. There were more than a hundred men in the ranks who had voluntarily met more dangers in their escape from slavery than any of my young captains had incurred in all their lives."

Another infantry unit from Worcester was the Massachusetts Twenty-First Regiment, which fought in some of the biggest battles of the Civil War, including Bull Run, Antietam, Chantilly, Roanoke Island, Fredericksburg and New Bern. It was notable for its connection to the Worcester area's own Clara Barton, one of the most famous women in American history. Barton was a war nurse who saved countless lives on the battlefield and later founded the American Red Cross, one of the world's leading humanitarian and disaster relief organizations.

Barton was born on December 25, 1821, in Oxford, Massachusetts, a town twelve miles south of Worcester. She grew up on a farm but took to nursing at an early age as she cared for her brother David, who fell off a barn roof and was laid up for nearly two years. However, since nursing was not a field that was open to women at the time, Barton went into teaching. She became a teacher at the age of eighteen in a school in her hometown of Oxford. A few years later, she started a school for the kids who worked at the local mill in town. She ran that school for several years and, during that time, taught many of the boys who would grow up to serve in the Twenty-First Regiment in the Civil War.

In 1851, after the family farm shut down, Barton moved to New York City to attend Clinton Liberal Institute, a prep school, to further her teaching career. She soon got a teaching job in Hightstown, New Jersey, and then founded the first public school in the neighboring town of Bordentown in 1852. But when she learned that the school hired a male principal at twice her salary to run the school she founded, she quit. "I may sometimes be willing to teach for nothing, but if paid at all, I shall never do a man's work for less than a man's pay," Barton reportedly said, according to the Clara Barton Missing Soldiers Office Museum.

Barton decided to leave the teaching profession and moved to Washington, D.C., where she got a job as a recording clerk in the U.S. Patent Office as part of President Franklin Pierce's administration. As the only woman in the office, she was harassed by the men who worked there. They tried to get her fired, but her boss saw through their tricks and not only kept her on staff but also paid her the same salary as the men, $1,400 a year, according to the National Women's History Museum. But when Pierce was defeated in the next presidential election and James Buchanan became president in 1857, Barton and most of the rest of the staff at the patent office were let go. Barton went back home to Oxford, but not for long. When Abraham Lincoln was elected president in 1860, she returned to her post in the U.S. Patent Office.

But then the Civil War broke out in 1861, and that changed everything for Barton. That April, Union soldiers arriving in Baltimore by train were mobbed and attacked by supporters of the Confederacy. The injured men were rushed to a makeshift hospital near the U.S. Capitol. Barton rushed over to help in any way she could, volunteering to provide food, clothing, medicine, supplies or whatever the wounded soldiers needed. As supplies were limited, she asked friends and relatives from back home to send the necessary items to her in Washington so that she could provide the proper care. Thus was the start of her career as the "angel of the battlefield."

Barton quit her job in the patent office as the war raged on, and she began visiting battlefields throughout Virginia, Maryland and the Carolinas, providing supplies and medical care for the wounded soldiers. Barton was on site at many of the major battles of the war, including Bull Run, Harpers Ferry, Chantilly, Antietam and Fredericksburg, according to the Clara Barton Birthplace Museum.

At Fredericksburg, Barton tended to soldiers from the Massachusetts Twenty-First Regiment, men from her hometown, many of whom she had taught in school. One of the men, Sergeant Thomas Plunkett, who lost both of his arms at Fredericksburg, credited Barton with saving his life. She later said the Twenty-First was her favorite, and they, in turn, adopted Barton as a daughter of the regiment, according to her biographer, Stephen Oates, author of *A Woman of Valor: Clara Barton and the Civil War*.

After the war, Barton continued in service to her country, establishing the federal Office of Missing Soldiers to find or identify soldiers who were either killed or missing in action. She wrote a letter to President Lincoln after the war, seeking permission to launch this initiative, which Lincoln immediately granted. The letter was published by the Clara Barton Missing Soldiers Office Museum.

To his Excellency Abraham Lincoln President of the United States
Sir, I most respectfully solicit your authority and endorsement to allow me to act temporarily as general correspondent at Annapolis Maryland, having in view the reception and answering of letters from the friends of our prisoners now being exchanged. It will be my object also to obtain and furnish all possible information in regard to those that have died during their confinement.

Clara Barton was an educator, a war hero, a nurse, a champion for women's rights and a pioneer for working women. But perhaps her greatest achievement came in 1881, when she founded one of the most important and enduring organizations in U.S. history, the American Red Cross. It was the culmination of a lifetime of service to the greater good.

Barton died on April 12, 1912, at her home in Glen Echo, Maryland. But her legacy lives on at the Clara Barton National Historic Site in Glen Echo, Maryland, the Clara Barton Missing Soldiers Office Museum in Washington, D.C., and the Clara Barton Birthplace Museum in her hometown of Oxford. And, of course, the American Red Cross.

Abbie Hoffman, shown circa 1969, a leader of the antiwar movement of the 1960s and '70s, grew up in Worcester. *Courtesy of Richard O. Barry, San Diego, California.*

As this book highlights, Barton is just one in a long line of radical reformers, revolutionaries and pioneers from the Worcester area in the nearly one hundred years from the American Revolution to the Civil War. That line did not end there but continued through the next one hundred years—and beyond.

Perhaps the stories of this next generation of reformers will be the subject of another book. But it should be noted that the line runs through the tumultuous 1960s to one of the leaders of the antiwar movement and the cultural revolution of that era, Abbie Hoffman, who grew up in Worcester. Hoffman was one of the renowned "Chicago Seven"—seven men who were charged with conspiracy and intent to incite a riot at protests in Chicago during the 1968 Democratic National Convention. Hoffman and the other defendants were ultimately acquitted in their famous trial. He was also the founder of the Youth International Party, or Yippies, and was one of the leaders of the "Flower Power" antiwar movement.

Hoffman was born in Worcester and attended the former Classical High School. He was a troublemaker and a prankster, and his irreverent antics got him expelled. He then enrolled at Worcester Academy and graduated in 1955. After attending college at Brandeis and graduate school at Cal-Berkeley, Hoffman moved back to Worcester to get married and work at Worcester State Hospital until 1966. That year, Hoffman moved to New York City and, like his Worcester lineage, sought to become a voice of change.

10

The Brief, Fascinating History of the Worcester Brown Stockings

In the summer of 2021, professional baseball made its triumphant return to Worcester with the debut of the Worcester Red Sox. The Triple-A affiliate of the Red Sox—just one step below the major leagues— moved to Worcester from its longtime home in Pawtucket, Rhode Island. While Worcester has hosted many other minor-league teams over the years, the WooSox, as they are called, is surely one of the most high-profile sports teams that has ever called Worcester home.

But it is not the *most* high-profile team to ever play in the city. That distinction belongs to the Worcester Brown Stockings, also known as the Worcesters and sometimes called the Ruby Legs. The Brown Stockings date back to the early days of the sport as one of the very first professional baseball teams, playing in the early days of the National League. Yes, Worcester was a major-league city.

The team actually wasn't even called the Brown Stockings during its brief existence from 1880 to 1882, nor was it called the Ruby Legs—that nickname seems to have been erroneously ascribed to the team over the years, as they had neither ruby nor red on their uniforms. The newspaper reports of the day referred to them simply as the Worcesters. That was a common descriptor at the time, as the Boston Red Stockings were often called the Bostons, the Chicago White Stockings were called the Chicagos, the Troy Trojans were referred to as the Troys and so on. But the Brown Stocking name seems to have stuck over the years, as the Worcester nine indeed donned brown stockings. I'll refer to them as both the Worcesters and the Brown Stockings. While the team's history is brief, it is certainly an interesting one, filled with historic moments, like the first-ever trip to Cuba by a professional baseball team and the first perfect game in baseball history.

The Worcester baseball franchise formed in 1879 as part of the International Association, a minor league that included two teams from Canada, thus the name. The timelines are a bit sketchy, but the International Association seems to have spun off from the National Association of Professional Base Ball Players, or the National Association, which is considered the first professional major league by many historians. The National Association existed from 1871 to 1875 and was dominated by the Boston Red Stockings—a team that would later become the Boston Braves and is now the Atlanta Braves.

The roots of the city's first professional team trace back to the Lynn Live Oaks, a team that played in the International Association. The league had thirteen teams, including two Canadian teams, Hornellsville and London. The rest of the league comprised Binghamton, Buffalo, Lowell, Lynn, Manchester, New Bedford, Pittsburgh, Rochester, Springfield, Utica and Syracuse.

The Lynn Live Oaks was managed by Hall-of-Fame pitcher William "Candy" Cummings, who was born in Ware, Massachusetts, and is credited as the first pitcher to throw a curve ball. But in the 1878 season, the team fell on hard financial times, and in the middle of the season, on June 4, the struggling Lynn team was forced to move to Worcester, a city with not only a great interest in the sport but also lots of local talent on the amateur level. Cummings left the team after the move to Worcester, and George Brackett finished out the season as the manager of the now Worcester Live Oaks. The team played the rest of the season at the Worcester Agricultural Fairgrounds, also referred to as the Driving Park, and finished with a record of 9-26.

It wasn't a successful half season in Worcester, but it opened the door for Worcester to be officially admitted to the league in 1879, only it was now called the National Association, as the two Canadian teams had disbanded. The Worcester club was one of nine teams in the National Association, along with squads from Albany, Rochester, Holyoke, Manchester, New Bedford, Springfield, Utica (Pent Ups) and Washington (Nationals). The team, called the Worcester Grays at the website Baseball Reference, played its full season of home games at the Agricultural Fairgrounds.

The Grays, or Worcesters, were owned by a group of local residents who formed the Worcester Base Ball Club, led by local businessman Martin

Flaherty, according to historian Charles Nutt. Former Worcester mayor Charles Pratt was also part of the ownership group. Flaherty's first move as owner was hiring Frank Bancroft as manager. Bancroft, who grew up in Lancaster, Massachusetts, was a true original and a baseball pioneer. He was considered a "prince of managers" in his time, according to Alan Foulds, author of *Boston's Ballparks and Arenas.*

Frank Bancroft, the first manager of the Worcester Brown Stockings. *Library of Congress Prints and Photographs Division.*

In his career, Bancroft went on to win the first World Series while managing the Providence Grays in 1884. It wasn't the first official World Series—that came in 1903, when the Boston Americans of the American League beat the Pittsburgh Pirates of the National League. But Bancroft's championship with the Grays is notable, because it was the first year that the National League champion, the Grays, played the champion of the American Association, the precursor to the American League. He also worked as a scout and executive for the Cincinnati Reds from 1892 to 1920, managing the team for one season in 1902. Bancroft was a good manager but an even better promoter, known as the first official to celebrate Opening Day with festivities and a ceremonial first pitch while with the Reds, according to baseball historian and author Charlie Bevis.

Bancroft came to baseball from the hotel business, having run the Benedict House hotel in New Bedford. While at the Benedict House, Bancroft managed a vaudeville comedy act called the Gleasons. It enabled him to earn enough money to open his own hotel, the Bancroft House in New Bedford, where he hosted a lot of vaudeville entertainers and theater performers, according to Bevis.

Recognizing the growing popularity of baseball, Bancroft built a baseball park in New Bedford, the Kempton Street Grounds. While amateur and semipro teams played there, New Bedford didn't have its own team to regularly fill it. So, Bancroft created one. His New Bedford team played in the National Association in 1878, against the Worcester Live Oaks. Bancroft treated the baseball team like it was a vaudeville touring group, booking some 130 games in 1878, far more than the other teams. On the Fourth of

July in 1878, he booked three games: a morning game in New Bedford, a game at noon in Taunton and a late-afternoon game in Providence.

It was this entrepreneurial spirit that caught the eye of Flaherty and the Worcester ownership group. Bancroft knew how to make money, and he knew how to promote the game, so they hired him to manage the Worcesters for a salary of $1,000, according to Bevis.

In 1879, their first full season in the National Association, the Worcesters went 26-26 and finished fifth in the league. It was a respectable record, but well behind the champion Albany Blue Stockings. Offensively, the Worcesters were led by their right fielder, Lon Knight, a native of Philadelphia. He batted .350 and had the most hits in the league with eighty-four. Outfielder Charlie Bennett, a native of New Castle, Pennsylvania, hit .328, while Doc Bushong, the catcher, from Philadelphia, hit .290. George Wood, an outfielder, hit a team-high .384 in limited games. Other key players on that team were shortstop Arthur Irwin and first baseman Chub Sullivan. Also, they had the services of one Jim Mutrie for that season. Mutrie went on to be the longtime manager of the New York Metropolitans in the American Association and later the New York Giants of the National League.

But their best player was pitcher Lee Richmond, a twenty-two-year-old from Sheffield, Ohio, who went to Brown University and led the school's team to the college baseball championship the previous year. Bancroft saw Richmond pitch at Brown and enticed the young hurler to pitch in an exhibition game for the Worcesters on June 2, 1879, against the Chicago White Stockings of the National League. Bancroft paid Richmond and his catcher, W.H. Winslow, ten dollars each for their services.

What happened next is the stuff of legend. Richmond pitched in that exhibition game against the mighty White Stockings, led by Cap Anson, the future Hall of Famer and the best player of his era. The White Stockings were 14-1 at the time and had won the National League in 1876. Richmond made them look like amateurs, throwing a no-hitter as Worcester beat the White Stockings, 11–0. It shocked the baseball world and made everyone take notice of Richmond and Worcester. This performance set off a bidding war for Richmond between Bancroft and Anson, who managed and played for the White Stockings. Bancroft was not the legend on the field that Anson was, but as a businessman, there were few better. He was able to close the deal and sign Richmond for $100 a month, explained baseball historian John Husman. Bancroft also allowed Richmond to continue pitching for Brown, which may have swayed Richmond to go with Worcester.

In the summer of 1879, Richmond led Brown to another college championship, beating Yale. Meanwhile, Richmond was also playing for Worcester. On June 11, he threw a two-hitter against the Washington Nationals and on July 28 pitched a no-hitter against Springfield. Between Worcester and Brown and all the exhibition games, Richmond won forty-seven games in 1879 as a pitcher and hit .350.

While they went 26-26 in the National Association in 1879, overall, including exhibitions, the Worcester nine compiled a record of 81-42-2. Against National League teams in exhibitions, the Worcesters went 6-5, with Richmond winning all of them and losing only twice. Among his signature wins, Richmond blanked the mighty White Stockings twice—by the scores of 11–0 and 5–0—and Providence once by the score of 5–0. At the end of the season, Bancroft signed Richmond to a contract for the 1880 season at a salary of $2,400 while he finished up his senior year at Brown, according to Husman.

The next season, 1880, would be a historic one for the Worcester Club. It started with a groundbreaking trip to play winter ball in Cuba and other parts south. These exhibition games would be the first to be played in Cuba by a team from the United States. This trip came about because Cuba was launching its first professional league in 1880, and officials wanted to make a big splash by inviting an established team from America to play against its best. It would not only promote the sport locally, but it would also put Cuba on the baseball map with the attention it got in America.

Cuban officials found two willing partners in Bancroft and Asa Soule, the owner of a company from Rochester, New York, that produced a medicinal tonic called Hop Bitters. Soule was also the owner of the National Association team the Rochester Hop Bitters. Soule saw this trip as a great opportunity to promote his elixir to a national and international audience. But his team, which had just done a barnstorming tour in California that fall, did not want to play.

Bancroft jumped at the chance to send his Worcester team, which was looking for an opportunity to do a barnstorming tour in the winter. The trip was set for December 1879, and the team would be called the Hop Bitters, even though nearly all the players, except one from Boston, would be from Worcester.

"Mr. Bancroft's nine composed entirely of the Worcesters of 1880, and whose names were given in our past issue, will leave this city on Dec. 13 and after visiting Havana, Cuba, will play on their way home at New Orleans, Galveston, Houston etc.," the *New York Clipper* reported on November 29, 1879.

Originally, the plan was to play the four leading clubs from Havana followed by a series of games against an all-star team of players from the four Cuban teams, reported the *Clipper*. But the trip did not go exactly as planned. Trouble brewed as soon as the team docked in Havana. The Cuban promoter who arranged the trip greeted them to say that their previous agreement of $2,000 plus half of gross receipts was null and void. The government said it would levy a 50 percent tax on gross receipts or they would not be allowed to charge admission. The tax would eat into the team's profits, but Bancroft was able to find a North American businessman on the island who agreed to fund their stay. However, the team was forced to cut back the schedule to only two games: one on Sunday, December 21, and the other on Sunday, December 28, with potentially two more on January 1 and 4.

The Worcester roster consisted of George Wood, Alonzo Knight, Charlie Bennett, Art Whitney, George Creamer, J.F. "Chub" Sullivan, C.J. "Curry" Foley, A.J. "Doc" Bushong, Arthur Irwin and Frederick "Tricky" Nichols. Foley of the Boston Red Stockings was the only non-Worcester player on the team. Some five thousand fans turned out for the game on December 21, which the Worcester club won easily, 21–7. A second game was to have been played later that week, but the Worcester squad determined that without the guarantee of the gate receipts, it did not make financial sense to stay any longer.

While the trip to Cuba was not profitable, it was a success, as it helped launch Cuba's baseball league and began a "continuous north–south exchange of talent and information" between the U.S., Cuba and other Caribbean nations that continues today, according to Adrian Burgos, author of the book *Playing America's Game: Baseball, Latinos, and the Color Line*. Bancroft led two more barnstorming trips to Cuba in 1908 and 1909 when he worked as business manager for the Reds. Through those trips, he was instrumental in bringing the first Cubans to the major leagues, Armando Marsans and Rafael Almeida, who joined the Reds in 1911, according to Burgos. Some even refer to Bancroft as the "father of Cuban baseball," wrote author Thomas Barthel in his book *Baseball Barnstorming and Exhibition Games, 1901–1962*.

The team boarded a ship bound for New Orleans on December 24 to continue their barnstorming tour through the southern United States. But when they arrived back home to Worcester later that winter, big news would be awaiting the team: an invitation to play in the National League.

In 1879, there were eight teams in the National League, including the Providence Grays, who won the title with a 59-25 record. They were followed in the standings by the Boston Red Stockings, Buffalo Bisons, Chicago White Stockings, Cincinnati Reds, Cleveland Blues, Syracuse Stars and Troy Trojans. The Stars, in their one and only year in the NL, failed to even finish the season due to financial hardships. They disbanded before the season ended, which created an opening for one team to join.

Three teams, all from the National Association, were in the running: the Worcesters, the champion Albany Blue Stockings and the Washington Nationals. Albany had been considered the favorite, as they were the best team in the National Association. But there was one small problem: the Blue Stockings didn't want to join, as the *Clipper* reported. "We have been informed authoritatively that the Albanys were wanted as the eighth member of the League, but that they declined to accept the invitation on the ground that it would be a suicidal policy on their part, as now they are at liberty to play all the League clubs that visit Troy, and at a reduced rate of admission." In other words, Albany could already play all the National League teams who came to nearby Troy in exhibitions and charge their own admission rates, not those dictated by the NL.

With Albany out of the running, Worcester was now the choice to replace the Syracuse Stars as a member of the National League. The Worcester club had a few things going for it, mainly their star pitcher, Richmond, who left quite an impression with his performance against NL clubs in exhibitions. Also, the team's financial situation was strong. Charles Pratt, the mayor of Worcester from 1877 through 1879 and a prominent local businessman, was now running the team as president. Pratt also was president of the Worcester County Agricultural Society, which owned the Worcester Agricultural Fairgrounds, where the team played.

Also, Worcester had the favor of National League president William Hulbert. The Worcesters were not only the most financially sound team in the NA, but they also appealed to Hulbert's conservative values. Hulbert had prohibited alcohol sales and consumption at games and banned playing Sunday games for religious reasons, and the Worcester ownership group championed both of these ideas, further endearing them to the league president, according to Bevis. Also, the league made "secret" agreements with Troy, Buffalo and Worcester to sell tickets at their own reduced rate to sweeten the pot, per the *Clipper*.

But there was one small problem: the city was not big enough. According to the National League charter, teams had to be from cities with a population of at least seventy-five thousand. Worcester, at the time, had around fifty-eight thousand people. For a team below that seventy-five-thousand threshold to be admitted, it needed unanimous support of all seven other teams. Worcester had the support of six teams, but not Troy, which wanted its neighbor, Albany. However, due to Hulbert's strong desire to get Worcester into the National League, the league amended the charter to include the population from within a four-mile radius of the city. When this was done, Worcester had the requisite population under the new parameters. So, on February 3, 1880, by a vote of 6–1, with Troy in dissent, Worcester was admitted to the National League, reported the *Clipper*.

There was a lot of excitement about the Worcester team. In its April 24, 1880 issue, the *New York Clipper* wrote a preview of the upcoming season. The author expected the Worcesters to be a team to be reckoned with. "We now come to the last team of all, but not by any means the least—and that is the new scholar In the League school, Bancroft's Worcester crowd. If what the Worcesters of 1879 accomplished against League teams in September and October last be any criterion, then this self-same Worcester team—strengthened in several points—is going to be well up in the race by the close of the season."

The Worcester club immediately got to work to prepare for the upcoming season. They held various fundraisers, including a concert by the Hyer Sisters, who were pioneers of Black musical theater. The Hyer Sisters produced the "first full-fledged musical plays…in which African Americans themselves comment on the plight of the slaves and the relief of Emancipation without the disguises of minstrel comedy." The team also held a ten-mile walking match, a five-mile road race and events at Mechanics Hall, as well as several other events to raise money and promote the team. In addition, ownership sold shares of the team for thirty-five dollars per share. Those who bought shares also got season tickets for forty-two home games, along with discount train fare and other perks, as baseball historian Charles Goslow detailed in his research project, "Fairground Days: When Worcester was a National League City, 1880–1882."

One big issue was the field. It may have been home sweet home for the Worcesters, but visiting teams were not fond of it. The diamond was placed in the middle of the horse track, as this park doubled as a driving park for horse races. According to Foulds's book, there was an actual tree growing in left field! It was definitely the most odd and unusual ballpark in the National League. The previous season, Providence complained about losing to Worcester in an exhibition game, citing the "semi-professional" condition of the field.

"The ball-ground was laid out inside the racecourse on a rough, broken field, remarkable for its pits and mounds, perfect traps for the unacquainted.

The infield was hobby, making it impossible for strangers to calculate anywhere near correctly on the bounds of the ball. The wretched condition of the grounds the Grays must owe their defeat. Time and again they would run the way they thought the ball would bound or roll and found too late that their calculations were wrongly made, and that the sphere was rolling far out into the field or else making caroms in acute angles. Thus, the Worcesters got base-hits which on any decent field would have resulted in dead outs," the *New York Clipper* reported on February 7, 1880, citing an account from a Providence paper.

The Providence paper surely used hyperbole when it claimed that Grays centerfielder Paul Hines "ran for a hit, and when last seen was knee-deep in a hole chasing a fly-ball."

Field conditions aside, the Agricultural Fairgrounds was a great place to watch a game. There was a wooden grandstand behind the backstop, but along both baselines, carriages could be driven and parked along the track. Fans were so close to the action and invested in the game that sometimes, according to Foulds, umpires asked the spectators for advice on calls. And it was a mixed crowd of both men and women, which was not always the case across the league, as women were not allowed to attend games in some cities. "The presence of ladies in the grandstands and in carriages outside the track gives character to the sport," wrote the *Spy*. But the fans could indeed get rowdy, as Goslow noted. In one game, a man was "thrown headlong down the seats, and another had his head mashed with a bottle."

There was a buzz in the city leading up to opening day. Bancroft himself opened a store on 34 Pearl Street in Worcester called the Baseball Emporium, which served as a gathering place for fans throughout the city. During the season, banners depicting the players were flown on lampposts on Main Street, and a scoreboard stood on the roof of the Friendly Clothing Store on Main Street to provide live updates for those who couldn't attend the game in person. Also, in a unique and perhaps groundbreaking promotion, the New England Telephone Company provided scores and game summaries to customers by phone for a twenty-five-cent charge, according to Goslow.

The Worcester club made their National League debut on May 1, 1880, against the team that didn't want them in the league, the Troy Trojans. The Worcesters won that game, 13–1, in front of about one thousand fans on a chilly spring day at the Agricultural Fairgrounds.

The Worcesters wore white flannel uniforms with brown trimming and brown stockings on opening day, lending credence to the Brown Stockings nickname that the team has been called over the years. However, it makes the Ruby Legs moniker, which has also stuck now for more than a century, difficult to understand. There is no reference to Worcester Ruby Legs in news articles of the day. The only near reference, as Foulds pointed out, is one in which the Worcesters lost to Boston and the headline said the Worcesters lost to the Ruby Legs, referring to the Red Sox as the Ruby Legs, not the Worcesters.

The Worcester colors were confirmed at a league meeting in December 1881. At that meeting, the committee on uniforms made a rule determining the new uniforms for the league. The *New York Clipper* reported: "The committee on uniforms—Messrs. Hulbert, Hotchkin and Winship—reported at second days session, and they adopted a special uniform for all the League teams, the only variation from which will be the 8 stockings, each club having a color of its own. Thus, the Chicago players will have white stockings; Cleveland, dark blue; Providence, light blue; Worcester, brown; Buffalo, gray; Troy, green; Boston, red; and Detroit, yellow."

On opening day, the Worcester Brown Stockings starting nine featured center fielder Harry Stovey batting leadoff, followed by left fielder George Wood, pitcher Lee Richmond, right fielder George Knight, third baseman Art Whitney, first baseman Chub Sullivan, shortstop Arthur Irwin, catcher Doc Bushong and second baseman George Creamer. Richmond got the win, allowing just one run on ten hits with three strikeouts. Wood had three hits, while Bushong, Stovey and Whitney each had two. The Worcesters won two of three from Troy and then swept their local rivals, the Providence Grays, in the next series to jump out to a 5-1 start, which put them in first place in the National League. It was the last time that season they were in first place, but there were more highlights to come.

On June 12, 1880, the young Worcester baseball franchise and their star pitcher, Lee Richmond, went into the record books, recording the first perfect game in major-league history. Richmond blanked the Cleveland Blues, 1–0, at the Agricultural Fair Grounds, outdueling Big Jim McCormick in front of seven hundred fans. Richmond allowed no hits, no walks and no runs, and the Worcesters made no errors. Not a single batter reached first base. It was what we now call a perfect game, but at the time there was no name for it, as no one had ever done it before. In his history of Worcester, author Charles Nutt called it a "no-hit, no-run game." The *Clipper* called it a "Splendid Pitching Game—An Unprecedented Score."

The *Worcester Evening Gazette* called it "the best baseball game on record." It was also the quickest game on record, lasting one hour and twenty-six minutes, including a seven-minute rain delay. As Jim Gates of the Baseball Hall of Fame recounted, the *Gazette* reported: "so faultless a game was rapidly played. It was half over in 45 minutes…the total time of one-hour and 26 minutes [made] the game one of the quickest ever played."

Making this historic feat even more impressive, on the morning of the perfect game, Richmond attended pre-graduation ceremonies at Brown University. He was set to graduate in just a few days, on June 16. That morning, he caught the 11:30 a.m. train from Providence to Worcester, rushed to the ballpark on an empty stomach and proceeded to make baseball history.

Years later, Richmond was asked about his perfect game. According to Gates, Richmond said: "It is a singular thing of that no-hit, no-run, no-man-reach-first game in 1880 that I can remember almost nothing except that my jump ball and my half stride ball were working splendidly and that the boys behind me gave me perfect support." The historic achievement is memorialized by a marker on the campus of Becker College, where the Agricultural Fairground once sat. It reads: "On June 12, 1880, the first perfect game in professional baseball history was pitched on this site (the former Worcester Agricultural Fairgrounds) by Lee Richmond of Worcester against Cleveland in a National League game."

The Brown Stockings had a respectable first campaign in the majors, going 40-43 with two ties to finish in fifth place in the league. They finished a half game ahead of the rival Boston Red Stockings, who were 40-44. Richmond finished fourth in the league in wins, going 32-32 on the year with a 2.15 ERA. He had five shutouts and 256 strikeouts. Baseball was a very different game back then, as most teams went with two or three pitchers, tops, which is why Richmond had so many starts. In fact, Richmond started sixty-six of the team's eighty-five games.

The team's leading hitter was Harry Stovey, who batted .265 and led the league in home runs with six, along with Boston's

The Brown Stockings' Harry Stovey led the National League in home runs in 1880. *Library of Congress Prints and Photographs Division.*

Jim O'Rourke. Other top hitters were Chub Sullivan (.259), shortstop Arthur Irwin (.259) and George Wood (.245). The Worcesters hit just .231 as a team, but they were one of the better fielding teams in the league, committing only 355 errors that first season, third best in the league. (It should be noted that fielders did not have gloves in 1880. Most fielding and catching was done with bare hands, as only the catcher and first baseman had gloves. Thus, errors were a huge part of the game. The fact that errors were far more common makes Richmond's perfect game all the more impressive.)

Their best defensive player was Irwin, who played shortstop and led the league with 345 assists. Three years later, while playing for Providence, Irwin would make history by introducing the glove to the sport among fielders. For Irwin, necessity was the mother of invention, as he had injured his hand and broke two fingers. Not wanting to miss any games, Irwin wore an oversized buckskin driving glove, padded it and sewed the third and fourth fingers together to allow space for bandages so that he could play, explained Eric Frost with the Society for American Baseball Research. Other players soon followed his lead. By the next season, 1884, almost every player in the league wore a fielding glove.

It was quite an eventful off-season for the Worcesters, as they were central players in a league-wide controversy and suffered an irreplaceable departure. The controversy involved the Reds getting kicked out of the league for flouting rules against selling alcohol at games and playing on Sundays.

The Worcesters were considered the most vocal complainers about the Reds' transgressions. It turned into a bitter battle between the two cities, Worcester and Cincinnati, led by the newspapers. The Worcester paper, the *Spy*, publicly railed against the Reds for selling alcohol at games and playing on Sundays. The *Cincinnati Inquirer* shot back in a July 17 editorial, "Puritanical Worcester." As quoted in Lee Allen's book *The Cincinnati Reds*, the editorial read: "Puritanical Worcester is not liberal Cincinnati by a jugful, and what is sauce for Worcester would be wind for the Queen City. Beer and Sunday amusements have become a popular necessity in Cincinnati."

The issue came to a head at the National League annual meeting in December. The league constitution was rewritten to strictly prevent the playing of any games at league parks on Sundays, even nonleague exhibition games. The policy now read that no "club shall take part in any game of ball on Sunday or shall allow any game of ball to be played on its grounds on Sunday," according to Michael Haupert with the Society of American Baseball Research. The Reds refused to comply. Team officials said they wouldn't stop selling beer or renting out the park on Sundays. As a result, the Reds were bounced from the National League.

The Reds would not play in the 1881 season, and it was a blemish on their record as the oldest continuously operating team in baseball history. But it was only a one-year hiatus. The Reds would be back in 1882, not with the National League, but as a charter member of the new American Association, which became a competing league that ran until 1901, when the American League was formed.

But the off-season took a turn for the worse when the team discovered that their manager and the driving force behind the team's success, Frank Bancroft, was leaving. Bancroft had become a hot property throughout the baseball world, not just for his skill as a manager but for his strength as a promoter and businessman. Also, it was believed that the Worcester owners did not want to re-sign Bancroft for the high salary he was seeking. Ownership felt they could do as well, and save money, with a player-manager, as many teams had done, as Bevis explained.

Bancroft signed on to manage the league's newest team, the Detroit Wolverines, which replaced the Reds. Making matters worse, Bancroft brought two of the Worcesters' best hitters, Lon Knight and George Wood, as well as catcher Charlie Bennett, to Detroit with him. Another huge loss on the field was John "Chub" Sullivan, their first baseman. He had become ill the previous season with consumption, later called tuberculosis. He would not be able to play in the 1881 season, and his teammates wore a black band on their uniforms in his honor. Sullivan died later that year, on September 12, at the age of twenty-five.

However, Bancroft left the team in good financial shape, and that allowed ownership to bring in some new faces to replace the departed players, namely Warren Carpenter from Cincinnati, Pete Hotaling from Cleveland and Lewis Dickerson from Troy. They also picked up Lip Pike, a four-time home run champ and all-time leader in home runs for the National Association. Pike, thirty-six, had been out of baseball for a few years, but he was trying to make a comeback. In addition, the Worcesters tapped Mike Dorgan from Providence as their player-manager.

Despite the rocky off-season, the team got off to a great start in 1881, winning their first eight games, including a three-game sweep of Bancroft and Detroit. They were 9-1 and in first place on May 17, but it all went downhill from there. The Brown Stockings lost ten of their next thirteen games to fall to 11-11. One of the few wins during that stretch was an 8–4 victory over Bancroft's visiting Detroit team before the largest crowd ever at the Fairgrounds, 3,652, according to Goslow.

A big problem was the fact that their ace, Richmond, was starting to wear down, having pitched so many innings over the past few years. It got to the point where Richmond asked for his release from the team in late July. As the losses mounted, infighting among the players grew. There was also conflict between the manager, Dorgan, and ownership, primarily team treasurer Freeman Brown, who had taken a more active role in running the team.

By August, the Worcesters had fallen into last place and Dorgan was fired, replaced temporarily by Stovey, one of the team's best players. The ownership team was able to convince Richmond to return to the team, but it didn't help much. The Brown Stockings finished the season in last place with a record of 32-50, twenty-three games behind first-place Chicago. Dickerson led the team with a .316 batting average, while Hotaling hit .309. Stovey hit .270 with a team-high seven triples and two home runs. Arthur Irwin hit .267. And despite his struggles, Richmond still had a solid year, with a record of 25-26 and a 3.39 ERA with three shutouts and 156 strikeouts. Not a bad record for a team that had a winning percentage of .390.

It was a frustrating end for a team that had gotten off to such a promising start. The Brown Stockings looked to turn the page on 1881 and make some big changes for the 1882 season. Freeman Brown, the team treasurer, was installed as the Worcesters manager for the 1882 season. Brown was also appointed to serve on the National League Board of Directors, which appeared to be a good sign for the team's longevity.

Brown decided to shake up the roster, given the insubordination, dysfunction and ineffective play that had marred the previous season. He brought back only six players from the previous season: Richmond, Stovey, George Creamer, Doc Bushong, Fred Corey and Arthur Irwin. Gone were Dickerson, Pike, Dorgan, Carpenter and Holating, among others. It was so bad that Dorgan, Dickerson and Lip Pike were actually blacklisted from the league for the 1882 season for "general dissipation and insubordination," as the *Boston Herald* reported on October 1, 1881. They were among nine players across the league who were blacklisted for the year by Hulbert.

The team vowed not to repeat the problems they had experienced in 1881 and issued a statement at its January 1882 meeting, as Goslow captured in *Fairground Days*. "Dissension, dissipation, and flagrant abuse of confidence made by some of the players brought about these results, professional baseball was now reduced to a business problem, and to be successful, the same principles must be applied to its management as are applied to any well-managed and successful corporation, woolen mill, or machine shop… there is no doubt that with a winning nine, Worcester will give first class support to baseball."

New players included Jake Evans, an outfielder from Troy; Jackie Hayes, a rookie catcher; pitchers Frank Mountain and Tommy Bond; and a rookie named John Clarkson. Baseball historians may recognize John Clarkson's name. When Clarkson, a pitcher from Cambridge, Massachusetts, joined the Worcesters, he was just a twenty-year-old rookie. He started only three games for Worcester and appeared in only four games that season, compiling a record of 1-2 with a 4.50 ERA. Clarkson won his first game as a starter on May 2, beating Boston, 11–10, but the rookie got roughed up in his next two starts. The team released him, signing Frank Mountain, who had played the previous year for Detroit, to replace him. It proved to be a bad move by the team, as Clarkson went on to become one of the best pitchers of his era. After leaving Worcester, he signed with the White Stockings and went on to win 328 career games, including an incredible 53 in 1885, his second season with Chicago. Only Charles Radbourn with Providence in 1884 ever won more games in a single season (59). Clarkson also had seasons in which he won 49, 38, 36 and 33 games. When he retired in 1894 with the Cleveland Spiders, he was the winningest pitcher in National League history. He was inducted into the Baseball Hall of Fame in 1963.

Unlike the previous two seasons, when the Brown Stockings got off to a fast start, the team stumbled out of the gates in 1882. Worcester lost seven of its first eight games, and to make matters worse, Richmond, with continued arm trouble, once again took a leave of absence. As the losses piled up, attendance kept dwindling. On July 11, the team was a dismal 9-32, and Brown took the blame, resigning as manager. At this point, the Worcesters were in dire financial straits due to dwindling attendance. The talk around the league was that the team would disband, but it staved off bankruptcy by raising enough funds during the season to stay afloat.

Bond had been a temporary pick as manager until a more permanent replacement could be found. He was manager for only six games, winning two of them. The board replaced Bond with John C. Chapman, who formerly managed at Holyoke in the National Association. The board realized that, after two unsuccessful seasons with player-managers, the team needed a full-time manager to run the team, perhaps recognizing their mistake in letting Bancroft go. But it didn't make much of a difference, as the team finished out the season with a record of 7-30 under Chapman. In the end, the Brown Stockings had a disastrous 18-66 record, finishing last in the National League by a wide margin.

In the final days of major-league baseball in Worcester, there were some highlights and some lowlights. As a highlight, they played in the major league's first ever doubleheader, on September 25, as baseball historian Charlie Bevis detailed in his book *Doubleheaders: A Major League History.* The Brown Stockings split the two games with Providence. Worcester won the first game, 5–4, while Providence took the second game, 8–6. The *Clipper* reported on this historic twinbill on October 7:

> *Worcester vs. Providence. The above-named clubs played two games Sept. 25 in Worcester, Mass. The one postponed from the preceding Friday was commenced at 1:30 p.m. and ended in an unexpected victory for the home-team owing to Farrell's fumbling….The second game began at 3:30 p.m., Carroll taking York's place with the visitors, while Richmond and Bushong pitched and caught for the home-team. Only eight innings were played on account of darkness. The Worcesters batted Radbourn very hard, Stovey leading off with a home-run, but they lost by errors made by Creamer and Bushong at critical points.*

On September 28, the Brown Stockings had a lowlight, hosting Troy in the lowest-attendance game in professional baseball history among games open to fans. The game attracted only six fans—yup, just six paying customers for a total gate of three dollars. "The game between these clubs Sept. 28 was marked by weak batting and brilliant fielding. The weather was very cold and raw, and the gross receipts at the gate were only $3. The Troys bunched their few hits and were again credited with a victory. Evans' fielding and Egan's batting were the chief features." Troy won, 4–1.

One day later, on September 29, the Brown Stockings played their last game as a major-league team, losing 10–7 to Troy. The crowd was only slightly higher, with twenty-five people in attendance. The *Clipper* reported on October 7, 1881: "The Worcesters and Troys finished their championship career in the League in the presence of about twenty-five people. Evans and Richmond exchanged positions, the former making his first appearance as pitcher in a League game. He pitched well but was poorly supported. The Troys took the lead at the outset, and, retaining it throughout, secured their sixth successive victory over the Worcesters." Fred Corey had three hits, while Irwin and Jake Evans each had two hits in this final game for the Brown Stockings.

These final games were so poorly attended because word had already been out for weeks that Worcester would no longer be part of the National League. Fans were rightfully upset and protested by refusing to show up. But there was some confusion about how that came about. At first, it was reported that both Worcester and Troy resigned from the league for lack of funding, as the *Clipper* reported on September 30. "The most important business of the meeting was the resignations of the Troy and Worcester Clubs, and the applications of the Metropolitan and Philadelphia Clubs to fill the vacancies. The principal reason given for the withdrawal of the two clubs was their want of success, both financially and in the contest for the championship."

The Worcester club felt it was being railroaded. Contrary to news reports, it had not agreed to voluntarily disband, as Worcester board member Fred Simester stated at a league meeting on September 12. But a vote was held later that month by the league to oust Troy and Worcester. "It is now denied that the Troy and Worcester Clubs voluntarily resigned their membership in the League. Director Simester of the Worcesters says that a resolution was adopted declaring it the sense of the meeting that these clubs be not represented in the association next season. The vote stood 6 to 2, Troy and Worcester of course voting in the negative," the *Clipper* reported on September 30, 1882. At the annual league meeting in December, it became official: the Worcester Brown Stockings were no more.

It was the league's contention that both Worcester and Troy were too small to support a team, particularly when the rival American Association had teams in major metropolitan areas. The two cities the National League eyed for replacing Worcester and Troy were Philadelphia and New York —major metropolitan areas. Another factor working against Worcester was the fact that NL commissioner Hulbert, who had always been a champion of the club, had recently died. With his death, his influence to save Worcester was gone.

The *Clipper* reported on December 16, 1882: "The delegates from Troy and Worcester, after listening to an explanation of the action taken in their case at the October meeting, tendered their clubs resignations as active members of the League, and the two clubs were then given the compliment of honorary membership in the League, with all the advantages that may pertain to the position—one, by the way, not known to the League constitution."

As an honorary member, they would be granted four exhibition games per year if they could field representative teams. Of course, exhibitions were quite common in those days—today, not so much. But who knows, maybe someday we will see the Brown Stockings again in an exhibition game. For now, all we have is their fascinating legacy.

Bibliography

Allen, Lee. *The Cincinnati Reds*. Kent, OH: Kent State University Press, 2006.

American Antiquarian Society. "Historical Notes Relating to the Second Settlement of Worcester." 1916. https://www.americanantiquarian.org.

————. "The News Media and the Making of America, 1730 to 1865" (exhibit). https://americanantiquarian.org.

American Battlefield Trust. "Ball's Bluff, Harrison's Island, Loudon County, Virginia, Oct. 21, 1861." www.battlefields.org.

————. "Fort Ticonderoga (1775). New York, May 10, 1775." www.battlefields.org.

Archives of Women's Political Communication. "Remarks at the Anti-Slavery Convention of American Women, May 17, 1838, Abby Kelley Foster." Iowa State University. https://awpc.cattcenter.iastate.edu.

Audretsch, Robert W., comp. *The Salem, Ohio 1850 Women's Rights Convention Proceedings*. Salem Area Bicentennial Committee and Salem Public Library, 1976.

Bacon, Margaret Hope. *I Speak for My Slave Sister: The Life of Abby Kelley Foster*. New York: Ty Crowell Company, 1974.

Barnes, George. "On Gettysburg Anniversary, Remembering Col. George Ward, Worcester's Brave Soldier." *Worcester Telegram*, July 2, 2013. https://www.telegram.com.

Barron, James. "Paul Revere, Beyond the Midnight Ride." *New York Times*, September 26, 2019.

Barthel, Thomas. *Baseball Barnstorming and Exhibition Games, 1901–1962.* Jefferson, NC: McFarland, 2007.

Baseball Reference. "1879 National Association." www.baseball-reference. com.

———. "Lynn Live Oaks." www.baseball-reference.com.

———. "National Association of Professional Base Ball Players." www. baseball-reference.com.

Bell, J.L. "Hancock's Trunk in Worcester, 16–22 Apr." Boston 1775. April 9, 2018. http://boston1775.blogspot.com.

Beveridge, Albert J. *Abraham Lincoln, 1809–1858.* Boston, MA: Houghton Mifflin, 1928.

Bevis, Charlie. *Doubleheaders: A Major League History.* Jefferson, NC: McFarland, 2010.

———. "Frank Bancroft." Society for American Baseball Research. https:// sabr.org.

———. "Worcester Nationals Ownership History." Society for American Baseball Research. https://sabr.org.

Bigelow Society. "Col. Timothy Bigelow." http://bigelowsociety.com.

Blackwell, Alice Stone. *Lucy Stone: Pioneer of Woman's Rights.* Charlottesville: University Press of Virginia, 2001.

Boston Herald. "The Creation of the Black List; Subject to Abuse." October 1, 1881.

Boston Public Library. *Letter from Thomas Wentworth Higginson, William Lloyd Garrison, Daniel Mann, and Wendell Phillips, Worcester, Massachusetts, 1857 July 8.* Digital Commonwealth. www.digitalcommonwealth.org.

Browne, Patrick. "Quock Walker and Emancipation in Massachusetts." *Historical Digression* (January 18, 2015).

Burgos, Adrian. *Playing America's Game: Baseball, Latinos, and the Color Line.* Berkeley: University of California Press, 2007.

Ceniza, Sherry. *Walt Whitman and the 19th Century Women Reformers.* Tuscaloosa: University of Alabama Press, 1990.

———. "The Woman's Rights Movement and Whitman." Walt Whitman Archives. https://whitmanarchive.org.

Chace, Elizabeth Buffum. *Anti-Slavery Reminiscences.* Central Falls, RI: E.L. Freeman & Son, State Printers, 1891.

Christensen, Robyn. "Gettysburg: One Family's Story." Worcester Historical Museum. www.worcesterhistory.org.

Clara Barton Birthplace Museum. *The Civil War.* www.clarabartonbirthplace. org.

Clara Barton Missing Soldiers Office Museum. Biography. www.clarabartonmuseum.org.

Colonial Society of Massachusetts. "February Meeting, 1937." www.colonialsociety.org.

Colvin, Kenneth. "Worcester Hero of the Revolution Died—in Jail!" Bigelow Society. 1998. http://bigelowsociety.com

Danvers Historical Society. *Old Anti-Slavery Days: Proceedings of the Commemorative Meeting, Held by the Danvers Historical Society.* Danvers, MA: Danvers Mirror Print, Danvers Historical Society, 1893.

Daughters of the American Revolution. "Colonel Timothy Bigelow Marker." www.dar.org.

———. Colonel Timothy Bigelow Chapter, Worcester. "The First School House in Worcester and John Adams, School Master." Worcester, MA: Commonwealth Press, 1903.

DiCanio, Teddi. "The Quock Walker Trials: 1781–83." Law Library—American Law and Legal Information. https://law.jrank.org.

Discover Central Mass. "Worcester Revolutionary Walking Tour." July 15, 2019. www.discovercentralma.org.

Douglass, Frederick. *The Life and Times of Frederick Douglass.* Boston, MA: De Wolfe & Fiske Company, 1892.

Duckett, Richard. "Mechanics Hall at Work on Portraits Project for Black Americans to Grace the Great Hall." *Worcester (MA) Telegram,* February 24, 2021. www.telegram.com.

Flower, Frank Abial. *History of the Republican Party.* Grand Rapids, MI: Union Book Company, 1884.

Force, Peter, ed. *American Archives: Containing a Documentary History of the English Colonies in North America, from the King's Message to Parliament of March 7, 1774, to the Declaration of Independence by the United States. Fourth Series.* Vol. 1. Washington, D.C.: Matthew St. Clair Clarke and Peter Force, 1837.

Foulds, Alan. *Boston's Ballparks and Arenas.* Lebanon, NH: University Press of New England, 2005.

Frost, Eric. "Arthur Irwin." Society for American Baseball Research. https://sabr.org.

Gardner (MA) News. "Commemorating Women's Rights Pioneer Lucy Stone." March 5, 2020.

Garrison, Wendell Phillips, and Francis Jackson Garrison. *William Lloyd Garrison, 1805–1879: The Story of His Life Told by His Children.* New York: Century Company, 1885.

Gates, Jim. "Lee Richmond Created Baseball Perfection." National Baseball Hall of Fame. https://baseballhall.org.

Goslow, Charles. "Fairground Days: When Worcester Was a National League City, 1880–1882." *Historical Journal of Massachusetts* 19, no. 2 (Summer 1991). Institute for Massachusetts Studies and Westfield State University.

Graves, Mary Hannah, Mary A. Stimpson and Martha Seavey Hoyt. *Sketches of Representative Women of New England*. Boston, MA: New England Historical Publishing Company, 1904.

Hackett, David. "The Rescue of John Hancock, Sam Adams, a Salmon, and a Trunk." Erenow. https://erenow.net.

Haupert, Michael. "William Hulbert and the Birth of the National League." Society of American Baseball Research. www.sabr.org.

Herndon, William. *Herndon's Life of Lincoln*. New York: World Publishing Company, 1930.

Hersey, Charles. *Reminiscences of the Military Life and Sufferings of Col. Timothy Bigelow*. Worcester, MA: Henry J. Holland, 1860.

Heywood, William Sweetzer. *The History of Westminster, Massachusetts*. Lowell, MA: S.W. Huse & Company, 1893.

Higginson, Mary Thacher. *Thomas Wentworth Higginson: The Story of His Life*. Boston, MA: Houghton Mifflin, 1914.

Higginson, Thomas Wentworth. *Army Life in a Black Regiment*. 1869. Reprint, Cambridge, MA: Riverside Press, 1900.

———. *Cheerful Yesterdays*. Cambridge, MA: Riverside Press, 1900.

———. "Emily Dickinson's Letters." *Atlantic Monthly* (October 1891).

———. *Massachusetts in Mourning: A Sermon, Preached in Worcester, on Sunday June 4, 1854*. Boston, MA: James Munroe and Co., 1854.

History.com. "Townshend Acts." https://www.history.com.

Hoar, George Frisbie. *Address Delivered Before the City Government and Citizens On the 200th Anniversary of Worcester, October 14, 1884*. Worcester, MA: C. Hamilton, 1885.

———. *Celebration of the Two Hundredth Anniversary of the Naming of Worcester, October 14 and 15, 1884*. Worcester, MA: Worcester City Council, 1885.

Hudson, Charles. *The Character of Abraham Lincoln: And the Constitutionality of His Emancipation Policy*. Boston, MA: Gale Cengage Learning, 1863.

Hunt, Gary. "The End of the Revolution and the Beginning of Independence: Social Upheaval in Colonial America—1774–1775 from Farmers to Patriots." Outpost of Freedom. February 2, 2010. www.outpost-of-freedom.com.

Hurd, Duane Hamilton. *History of Worcester County, Massachusetts*. Vol. 3. Philadelphia, PA: J.W. Lewis & Company, 1884.

Husman. John. "June 2, 1879: Lee Richmond's No-Hit Debut." Society of American Baseball Research. https://sabr.org.

———. "Lee Richmond." Society of American Baseball Research. https://sabr.org.

Irvin, Benjamin H. "Tar, Feathers, and the Enemies of American Liberties, 1768–1776." *New England Quarterly* 76, no. 2 (June 2003).

Jarvis, Tim. "Liberty Farm." New Worcester Spy. November 15, 2016. http://newworcesterspy.net.

Kerr, Andrea Moore. *Lucy Stone: Speaking Out for Equality*. New Brunswick, NJ: Rutgers University Press, 1992.

Kinsmen and Kinswomen. "The Dedication of the Timothy Bigelow Monument in Worcester." July 20, 2016. https://kinsmenandkinswomen.com.

———. "The Life of Timothy Bigelow, Crowdsourced." July 29, 2016. https://kinsmenandkinswomen.com.

LaMar, Susan G. *The Poetry, Politics, and Prophecy of Abby Hills Price*. Published by Hope, 1842.

Law Library—American Law and Legal Information. "Levi Lincoln." https://law.jrank.org.

Lewis, J.W. *The History of Worcester, Massachusetts*. Philadelphia, PA: J.W. Lewis, 1889.

Library of Congress. Abraham Lincoln Papers. Series 1. General Correspondence. 1833–1916: Charles Hudson to Abraham Lincoln, Tuesday, November 13, 1860. www.loc.gov.

———. Abraham Lincoln Papers. Series 1. General Correspondence. 1833–1916: Charles Hudson to Abraham Lincoln, Wednesday, July 10, 1861. www.loc.gov.

———. "James Madison to Levi Lincoln, January 20, 1811." www.loc.gov.

———. "Massachusetts Constitutional Convention No. 97. July 1, 1853." www.loc.gov.

———. *Proceeding of the Anti-Slavery Convention of American Women, Held in Philadelphia, May 15th, 16th, 17th and 18th, 1838*. https://www.loc.gov.

———. *The Proceedings of the Woman's Rights Convention, held at Worcester, October 15th and 16th, 1851*. New York: Fowlers and Wells, 1852. https://www.loc.gov.

———. *The Proceedings of the Woman's Rights Convention, held at Worcester, October 23rd and 24th, 1850*. Boston, MA: Prentiss and Sawyer, 1851.

———. "Thomas Jefferson to Levi Lincoln, December 28, 1804." www.loc. gov.

Lincoln, William. *History of Worcester, Massachusetts: From Its Earliest Settlement to September 1836 with Various Notices Relating to the History of Worcester County*. Worcester, MA: M.D. Phillips, 1837.

Livermore, George. *An Historical Research Respecting the Opinions of the Founders of the Republic on Negroes as Slaves, as Citizens, and as Soldiers. Read before the Massachusetts Historical Society. August 14, 1862*. Boston, MA: A. Williams and Company, 1863.

Lovell, Albert Alonzo. *Worcester in the War of the Revolution: Embracing the Acts of the Town from 1765 to 1783 Inclusive*. Worcester, MA: Tyler & Seagrave, 1870.

Marvin, Abijah Perkins. *History of Worcester County, Massachusetts: Embracing a Comprehensive History of the County from Its First Settlement to the Present Time, with a History and Description of Its Cities and Towns*. Vol. 1. Boston, MA: C.F. Jewett and Company, 1879.

———. *History of Worcester in the War of the Rebellion*. Worcester, MA: self-published, 1880.

Massachusetts Historical Society. "Declaration of Independence: Independence Declared in Boston." https://masshist.org.

———. *Proceedings of the Massachusetts Historical Society* 48 (1915).

———. *Proceedings of the Massachusetts Historical Society* 6 (1863).

———. "The Ratification of the U.S. Constitution in Massachusetts." 2002. https://www.masshist.org.

———. *The Second National Woman's Rights Convention Worcester, MA October 15–16, 1851*. https://www.masshist.org.

Massachusetts Law Updates (blog). "Massachusetts Declaration of Rights—Article 1." January 1, 2019. https://blog.mass.gov.

Massachusetts Provincial Congress. *The Journals of Each Provincial Congress of Massachusetts in 1774 and 1775*. Boston: Dutton and Wentworth, Printers to the State, 1838.

Mass Moments. "First National Women's Rights Convention Ends in Worcester, October 24, 1850." www.massmoments.org.

McClymer, John F. *This High and Holy Moment: The First National Women's Right's Convention, Worcester, 1850*. San Diego, CA: Harcourt Brace College Publishers, 1999.

———. *U.S. Women's History Workshop*. Assumption College. Worcester, Massachusetts.

McClymer, John, Lucia Knoles and Arnold Pulda, co-directors. E Pluribus Unum Project. "The Fugitive Slave Case in Boston." Assumption College. Worcester, Massachusetts. http://www1.assumption.edu.

Michals, Debra. "Clara Barton, 1821–1912." National Women's History Museum. www.womenshistory.org/education-resources/biographies/clara-barton

———. "Lucy Stone, 1818–1893." National Women's History Museum. Alexandria, Virginia, 2017. www.womenshistory.org.

Miller, Marion Mills, and Francis Bicknell Carpenter. *The Works of Abraham Lincoln*. Vol. 2. New York: C.S Hammond and Company, 1908.

Moore, Frank. *The Diary of the Revolution: A Centennial Volume Embracing the Current Events in Our Country's History from 1775 to 1781 as Described by American, British, and Tory Contemporaries*. Hartford, CT: J.B. Burr & Company, 1876.

Moynihan, Kenneth J. *A History of Worcester, 1674–1848*. Charleston, SC: The History Press, 2007.

National Baseball Hall of Fame. "Candy Cummings." https://baseballhall.org.

National Gallery of Art. "Robert Peckham and His Portraits of Children." https://www.nga.gov.

National Park Service. "In Defense of Woman and the Slave." Women's Rights, National Historical Park. www.nps.gov.

———. "Lucy Stone." Women's Rights National Historical Park. www.nps.gov.

———. "More Women's Rights Conventions." www.nps.gov

National Pastime. "A Perfect Place, Worcester, MA. Roadside Recollections: Off the Beaten Baseball Path." www.nationalpastime.com.

Neuman, Johanna. *And Yet They Persisted: How American Women Won the Right to Vote*. New York: Wiley, 2019.

New England Historical and Genealogical Society. *New England Historical and Genealogical Register* 51. Boston, Massachusetts, 1897.

New England Historical Society. "Abby Kelley Shakes Up Seneca Falls." https://www.newenglandhistoricalsociety.com.

———. "The Speech That Set the Women's Rights Movement on Fire." https://www.newenglandhistoricalsociety.com.

New York Clipper. "Baseball." November 22, 1879. Illinois University Digital Newspaper Collections. https://idnc.library.illinois.edu.

———. "Baseball." November 29, 1879.

———. "Baseball." January 24, 1880.

———. "Baseball." February 7, 1880.

———. "Baseball." February 14, 1880.

———. "Baseball." April 24, 1880.

———. "Baseball." May 8, 1880.

———. "Baseball." June 19, 1880.

———. "Baseball." December 17, 1881.

———. "Baseball." July 22, 1882.

———. "Baseball." September 30, 1882.

———. "Baseball." October 7, 1882.

———. "Baseball." December 16, 1882.

———. "The Worcesters Southern Tour." January 10, 1880.

Nichols, Charles Lemuel. *Isaiah Thomas, Printer, Writer & Collector.* Cambridge, MA: Harvard University, 1912.

Nutt, Charles. *The History of Worcester and Its People.* Vol. 1. New York: Lewis Historical Publishing, 1919.

Oates, Stephen. *Woman of Valor: Clara Barton and the Civil War.* New York: Free Press, 1995.

Oleson, Ellie. "Barton Mills Are Being Unearthed by Local Man." *Worcester Telegram*, August 13, 2009.

Otis, James. *1763: Otis, Rights of British Colonies Asserted* (pamphlet). Online Library of Liberty. https://oll.libertyfund.org.

Parkman, Ebenezer. "The Diary of Rev. Ebenezer Parkman." The Ebenezer Parkman Project. http://diary.ebenezerparkman.org.

Project Ballpark. "Driving Park at Agricultural County Fair Grounds." www.projectballpark.org.

Raphael, Ray. *The First American Revolution: Before Lexington and Concord.* New York: New Press, 2002.

———. "Instructions: The People's Voice in Revolutionary America." *Commonplace: The Journal of Early American Life* (October 2008).

———. "The True Start of the American Revolution." *Journal of the American Revolution* (February 12, 2013).

Revolutionary Worcester. "Hancock House." April 13, 2020. https://revolutionaryworcester.org.

Rice, Franklin Pierce. *Dictionary of Worcester, Massachusetts and its Vicinity.* Worcester, MA: F.S. Blanchard & Company, 1889.

Rodrique, Jessie M. "Why Worcester? Excerpt from Worcester Women's Heritage Trail." Worcester Women's History Project, 2002.

Rugg, Arthur Prentice. *Abraham Lincoln in Worcester.* Worcester, MA: Belisle Printing and Publishing Company, 1914.

Siebert, William. *The Underground Railroad in Massachusetts*. Worcester, MA: American Antiquarian Society, 1935.

Smith, Henry. *Charles Hudson In Memoriam: A Paper Read at the Meeting of the Worcester Society of Antiquity, May 17, 1881*. Worcester, MA: Snow, Woodman and Company, 1881.

Some Historic Houses of Worcester. Worcester, MA: Worcester Bank and Trust Company, 1919.

Spears, John Pearl. *Old Landmarks and Historic Spots of Worcester, Massachusetts*. Worcester, MA: Commonwealth Press, 1931.

State Disunion Convention. *Proceedings of the State Disunion Convention, Held at Worcester, Massachusetts, January 15, 1857*. Boston, MA: Printed for the Committee, 1857.

Statmuse, Worcester Ruby Legs, 1881 Regular Season Game Results." www.statmuse.com.

Stats Crew. "1878 Lynn Live Oaks/Worcester Worcesters Statistics." www.statscrew.com.

———. "1879 National Association. Worcester, Roster and Statistics." www.statscrew.com.

Stone, Lucy, and Antionette Brown Blackwell. *Friends and Sisters: Letters between Lucy Stone and Antoinette Brown Blackwell, 1846–1893*. Champaign: University of Illinois Press, 1987.

Stone Sentinels. "The Battle of Gettysburg, George H. Ward." http://gettysburg.stonesentinels.com.

Tarbell, Ida M. "The Life of Lincoln." *McClure's Magazine* (January 1896).

Taylor, Zachary. *The True Whig Sentiment: General Taylor's Two Allison Letters*. Boston, MA: Eastburn's Press, 1848.

Thomas, Isaiah. *The Diary of Isaiah Thomas, 1805–1828*. Edited by Benjamin Thomas Hill. Worcester, MA: American Antiquarian Society, 1909.

USHistory.org. "Declaration of Independence: Massachusetts Government Act." www.ushistory.org.

Wall, Caleb Arnold. *Reminiscences of Worcester from the Earliest Period, Historical and Genealogical, with Notices of Early Settlers and Prominent Citizens, and Descriptions of Old Landmarks and Ancient Dwellings*. Worcester, MA: Tyler & Seagrave, 1877.

Waxman, Olivia B. "Lucy Stone, If You Please: The Unsung Suffragist Who Fought for Women to Keep Their Maiden Names." *Time*, March 7, 2019.

Worcester Historical Museum. "Age of Reform." https://www.worcesterhistory.org.

Worcester Magazine. "A Clover for Emily: Love, Life and Loss for Worcester Civil War Family." February 9, 2018. https://www.worcestermag.com.

Worcester Women's History Project. "Why Commemorate the 1850 Woman's Rights Convention?" www.wwhp.org.

About the Author

D ave Kovaleski has been a writer, editor and reporter for more than thirty years, working for a variety of organizations, including Standard & Poor's, Penton Media, Crain Communications, Crane Data, Macallan Communications and the Motley Fool. Dave lives in central Massachusetts with his wife and two kids. He has always been fascinated by local history and learning about the people and events that shaped our communities. This is his first book for The History Press.

Visit us at
www.historypress.com